COOPERATION IN THE CLASSROOM:

Students and Teachers Together
SECOND EDITION

James S. Cangelosi

DISCARD

nea PROFESSIONAL LIBRARY
National Education Association
Washington, D.C.

To Anna Marie and Rosario
who taught me to be original.

To Allison, Amanda, Amy, Casey, and Chris
who taught me what is important.

To Barb
who taught me love.

Printing History
   First Printing: August 1984
   Second Printing: July 1986
   SECOND EDITION: January 1990

Note

The opinions expressed in this publication should not be construed as representing the policy or position of the National Education Association. Materials published by the NEA Professional Library are intended to be discussion documents for teachers who are concerned with specialized interests of the profession.

Library of Congress Cataloging-in-Publication Data

Cangelosi, James S.
   Cooperation in the Classroom : students and teachers together /
James S. Cangelosi.—2nd ed.
      p. cm. — (Analysis and action series)
   Includes bibliographical references.
   ISBN 0-8106-3072-9
   1. Classroom management. 2. Teacher-student relationships.
3. Interaction analysis in education. I. Title. II. Series.
LB3013.C326 1990
371.1 023—dc20   89-38913
                                               CIP

CONTENTS

The Author

James S. Cangelosi is Associate Professor of Education, Department of Secondary Education, College of Education, Utah State University, Logan.

The Advisory Panel

Ruth W. Bauer, English teacher, Dodd Junior High School, Cheshire, Connecticut

Earl D. Clark, University of Alaska, Juneau

Lawrence M. Hoffman, Fort Worth Independent School District, Texas

Marilyn Louwerens, IMTS Coordinator, George Stone Vocational Center, Pensacola, Florida

Donald D. Megenity, Professor of Psychology, University of Southern Colorado, Pueblo

Eula Ewing Monroe, Associate Professor, Western Kentucky University, Bowling Green

Judy Reinhartz, Associate Professor and Assistant Director for Field Experiences, Center for Professional Teacher Education, University of Texas at Arlington

Beverly G. Schuh, Home Economist, Ashley High School, North Dakota

Martha Stanfill, fifth grade teacher, Chaffee School, Huntsville, Alabama

Ray Taylor, mathematics teacher, Waynesboro High School, Georgia

Joyce G. Temby, mathematics and Spanish teacher, Los Cerros Intermediate School, Danville, California

AUTHOR'S PREFACE
TO THE SECOND EDITION

Keeping students engaged in learning activities and on task and effectively dealing with off-task and disruptive student behaviors generally present teachers with their most perplexing challenges (99; 117, pp. 5–9; 125).* Overwhelmingly, teachers indicate that problems in the area of classroom management and student discipline presented them with their greatest difficulties and led to feelings of inadequacy during their first two years of teaching (94, 103, 115). According to studies conducted over the past seventy-five years, improper management of student behavior is the leading cause of teacher failure (90, p. 5).

Teachers can justifiably "blame" students' inattentiveness, lack of effort, disruptive behavior, and general lack of cooperation on students' personality traits or on the lack of support provided by society, families, and school administrators. But even in the face of unfavorable attitudes and conditions, teachers *can* still manage to overcome seemingly impossible circumstances and elicit students' attention, effort, and cooperation. How can middle and secondary school teachers achieve such results? This is the question addressed by *Cooperation in the Classroom: Students and Teachers Together*.

The first five chapters of this book focus on ways for teachers to manage time and space, plan lessons, establish classroom rules and procedures, and communicate with students that enhance the chances that students will cooperate and discipline problems will be avoided. Chapter 6 suggests ways of effectively responding to student misbehaviors and lack of engagement in lessons. In this second edition, Chapter 6 has been revised and expanded from the first edition to include additional suggestions and more examples. In consideration of the alarming rate of drug abuse among students that interferes with their ability and willingness to be engaged in lessons (114, 121), a section addressing this problem is included.

The suggestions for teachers in this book are an outgrowth of both direct classroom experiences and the findings of numerous studies related

---

*Numbers in parentheses appearing in the text refer to the Bibliography beginning on page 71 and to the Additional References for the Second Edition beginning on page 77.

to behavior management, student engagement, and time on task. The ideas presented are drawn from a variety of classroom discipline approaches.

Jacob Kounin's (91, pp. 15–19; 98, pp. 27–39; 110) approach emphasizes the following teacher characteristics and abilities that affect students' cooperation: (1) being aware of what is going on in their classrooms, (2) handling one problem behavior in a way that positively influences other behaviors, (3) making smooth transitions from one classroom activity to another, (4) dealing concurrently with a number of classroom events, and (5) maintaining the group's focus on a single task or topic.

Frederic Jones (45; 97, pp. 88–102) emphasizes the following factors: (1) the teacher's use of body language to communicate expectations to students, (2) whether or not incentives for cooperation are truly valued by students, (3) the efficiency with which time is used to provide help to students, and (4) the physical proximity of the teacher to students during a lesson.

Offering solutions to common communications problems between students and teachers, Haim Ginott (35; 91, pp. 23–25) suggests that teachers (1) use descriptive instead of judgmental language styles, (2) focus on situations and behaviors rather than on personalities, (3) model behaviors that are expected of students, and (4) be extremely cautious in their use of praise.

Lee and Marlene Canter (17; 91, pp. 29–33, 199–203) suggest that teachers (1) use an assertive response style that is neither passive nor hostile, (2) not confuse understanding misbehavior with excusing it, (3) develop and follow a plan for encouraging student behavior that is desirable and discouraging that which is undesirable, and (4) seek and expect support from parents and school administrators.

William Glasser (36, 104, 105, 106) emphasizes (1) teaching students to make appropriate behavior choices, (2) establishing and enforcing rules of conduct, and (3) holding students accountable for their own behaviors.

Rudolph Dreikurs (26, 27) stresses that teachers should be neither autocratic nor permissive if they expect students to be cooperative in the classroom. Dreikurs related student misbehaviors to their mistaken ideas about how to attain acceptance and approval of peer groups.

The Teacher Effectiveness Training of Thomas Gordon (38; 128, pp. 26–45) emphasizes (1) the recognition that each person is responsible for her/his own problems and (2) the value of teachers actively listening to students and using supportive replies.

6

The behaviorist approach (14, 53) provides explanations as to why students develop both desirable and undesirable habits of conduct. The techniques for helping students develop cooperative behavior patterns and suppress those that are uncooperative are based on principles of positive reinforcement, punishment, negative reinforcement, modeling, satiation, shaping, schedules of reinforcement, generalization, and discrimination (91, pp. 215–31).

In addition, the numerous time-on-task studies (31, 45) also influenced this book. These studies provide teachers with a proverbial "bad news" and "good news" story. There are disappointing indications that middle and secondary school students average no more than 25 percent of their school time engaged in learning activities. The time-on-task studies are encouraging, however, because they show that the application of some basic classroom organization and time management techniques can lead to a tripling of the time students spend actively engaged in learning activities.

Thousands of students and teachers with whom I have worked over the past twenty-four years have had an impact on the thoughts that went into this work. I am most grateful to them as I am to Barb Rice, who served as my copyreader and adviser, and who remained nearby to continually remind me of the everyday realities of classroom teachers working in less-than-ideal circumstances.

Chapter 1

FINDING YOURSELF

Nobody can be taught faster than he can learn. . . . Every man that has ever undertaken to instruct others can tell what slow advances he has been able to make, and how much patience it requires to recall vagrant inattention, to stimulate sluggish indifference, and to rectify absurd misapprehension.

—Samuel Johnson, *Life of Milton*

Suppose with me for one terrible moment that you can not only see and hear your students while you are conducting lessons, but you can also read their thoughts. Now further imagine that, while leading a discussion session during a particular lesson, with your newly acquired mind-reading ability you observe the following three students:

1. Valerie is quite bored with the lesson and is carrying on a lively conversation with her friend Betty about the TV show that she watched last night.

2. Laura looks at you attentively; her thoughts are filled with admiration for you. She is not concentrating on the discussion so much as she is concerned with leaving a positive impression on you and receiving high marks.

3. Katrina is listening intently to what you and other students are saying. She struggles to formulate answers to questions that are raised in the discussion. She doesn't concern herself with thoughts of you or the quality of the lesson.

With which one of the three students do you feel most successful? Be honest with yourself. I hope your answer is Katrina. Her participation should maximize the lesson's benefits for her.

A student like Katrina, who is participating in a lesson in the manner in which it was designed, is said to be "on task" (48) or "engaged" (31) in the lesson. A student like Laura, who is not involved and participating in a lesson as it was designed, is said to be "off task" (35) or "disengaged" (9) in the lesson. A student like Valerie, who is not only off task but is also preventing other students from being on task, is said to be "disruptive."

While it is highly unusual for a teacher to prefer students to be disruptive, unfortunately many teachers are not committed to maintaining student engagement (13). Here is an example:

In attempting to explain a solution to a problem in class, Mr. McDonald says, "...so we know that y has to be larger than x." Amy interrupts: "But can't the square of a number be less than the number?" "Of course not," Mr. McDonald replies. Amy: "But the square of one-half is one-fourth and one-fourth is less than one-half. Isn't it?" Mr. McDonald feels a rush of embarrassment in front of the class. He experiences no satisfaction with Amy's astute observation because he feels that she has made him appear "stupid." He resents her observations and tries to mask his embarrassment and resentment by focusing on the fact that she interrupted him. "Amy, you know you shouldn't talk out without first being recognized," he snaps. "I know that one-half squared is one-fourth, but we were talking only about whole numbers. That's something you weren't supposed to know yet." Amy: "Yes, sir."

Amy becomes quiet and does not interrupt again. Although she is not disruptive, she is no longer engaged in the lesson. She does not listen to the mathematical explanations as she continues to think about Mr. McDonald's anger.

Because Mr. McDonald continues to feel embarrassed, his explanations become more rambling and he repeats himself. The students sit politely and think about other things.

A school principal walking into the classroom just after Mr. McDonald "put Amy in her place" would see no disruptive behavior and might think that the class was quite attentive. However, teachers like Mr. McDonald, who feel compelled to display their superiority over students, are unlikely to maintain high levels of student engagement (35).

Where do your priorities lie? How committed are you to maintaining high levels of engagement for all your students? Do you feel just as responsible for helping those who seem bored and unimpressed as you do for helping those who seem to hang on to every word you utter?

This book can help you achieve greater cooperation from all the students in your classroom. It offers classroom-tested strategies that can decrease the incidence of disruption and also increase student engagement in your lessons.

WHO OR WHAT IS RESPONSIBLE FOR STUDENTS' CLASSROOM BEHAVIOR?

What causes students to be off task—either disruptively or nondisruptively—when they should be engaged in lessons? Some teachers with whom I raised this question emphasized factors over which they had no control. Here are some of their responses:

- Two of my students were so stoned in class today that they couldn't think straight. This happens because there are drug dealers all over this town.

- Jim talked incessantly during a silent reading session today because the classes at our school are too large for anyone to maintain order.

- Arlette failed to do her homework assignment because her parents let her watch television all night instead of encouraging her to do schoolwork.

- Charlene and Marion are more interested in each other than they are in history, so they talked to each other instead of listening to my history lecture.

Any undesirable, off-task behavior that a student exhibits while under the direction of a teacher can be "blamed" on the student or on causes outside the teacher's domain. But both the student and the teacher are responsible for the student's engagement or lack of engagement in a lesson. It is tempting to focus the "blame" for off-task behaviors on society, television, parents, or other factors. Too-large classes, excessive paperwork required by administrators, unexpected interruptions (such as band members being called out of the classroom during a lesson), uncooperative parents, time-consuming school board regulations, student access to debilitating drugs, lack of suitable equipment—these may be only a few of the obstacles that make it difficult for teachers to keep students engaged in their lessons. It is of course important to work to eliminate such factors. Nevertheless, until all the battles are won, teachers need to focus on what they can do to keep students engaged and on task even in the face of these constraints.

This book does not provide you with solutions for reducing class size, making administrators more responsive to your needs, or ridding society of drugpushers. It does, however, suggest techniques that you can use to keep students engaged in lessons, techniques that you can apply in spite of the unfavorable conditions under which you may operate.

In many situations, off-task behavior is more ''normal'' for students than engaged behavior. For example, in the last response cited, Marion and Charlene's greater interest in each other than in history is not only expected, but it is often considered healthy. In fact, off-task behavior such as relaxing is sometimes more natural for students than is absorption in taking lecture notes. Thus the more useful question for teachers may be, What causes students to become engaged in lessons?—rather than, What causes them to be off task?

Chapter 2

MANAGING TIME AND SPACE

By doing nothing, men learn to do evil.

—Columella, *De rustica*

We shape our buildings; thereafter, they
shape us.

—Winston Churchill

USING STUDENTS' TIME EFFICIENTLY

Mr. Grah, a teacher of 28 seventh graders, plans to conduct an activity in which students work in pairs with $60 in play money. His lesson goes as follows:

The students begin to file into Mr. Grah's room after lunch. The noise level is what one would expect for such a situation. Mr. Grah waits for everyone to be seated and quiet down somewhat. Then he raises his voice slightly to give the following directions: "All right! I want you to find yourselves a partner . . . You and your partner should sit next to each other at a worktable." With some jockeying the students shuffle to be with the partners of their choice. Initially some students have no partners and others have two. After a few incidents with such comments as "Why do I have to be with David? I always get stuck with David!" and "I wanna be with Barbara!" the students settle down with partners at the worktables. The process uses 11 minutes. A little concerned over the confusion, Mr. Grah speaks louder than before, "I am going to pass out $60 to each pair." As he begins to count and distribute the play money, students react with questions and remarks such as "What are we going to do?" "Oh! I thought it was going to be real money!" "Mr. Grah, you gave us only $50!" It takes the teacher 15 minutes to distribute the desired amount to each set of partners, during which time instances of off-task conversations, doodling, and daydreaming occur. Mr. Grah gives directions for the lesson, but by then several students have lost interest and about 30 minutes have elapsed. (16)

Like Mr. Grah, Ms. Hernandez teaches 28 seventh graders. She also wants to conduct the same activity with her class that Mr. Grah conducted. However, she prepares for her class with greater care. Before the students enter the room, Ms. Hernandez places 14 different numerals (for example, "58") at each of 14 work stations that she has set up. She has also prepared 28 five-by-eight-inch cards (one for each student) similar to the card pictured in Figure 1. The numbers at the top of each card are to be computed. These numbers have been selected so that each card has only one matching answer among the other cards. For example, a card with "1566/27" at the top would match only the one shown in Figure 1. Thus the students who obtained these two cards would be partners at station "58."

FIGURE 1
ONE OF MS. HERNANDEZ'S 28 5 x 8-INCH CARDS

29 × 2

Go to the place at the worktable that has a number equal to the number at the top of this card. There you will meet your partner. After you and your partner arrive and are seated at the table, locate the envelope taped under the table top. Remove the envelope and open it. Inside you will find $60 in play money and instructions on what you and your partner should do with it. Good luck!

Ms. Hernandez determines who will be partners with whom by placing one card on each person's desk before the students arrive in the classroom. Her selection keeps "troublemakers" apart, matches students who work well together, and takes advantage of student personality traits of which she is aware. The lesson goes as follows:

14

The students begin to file into the room after lunch. The noise level is what one would expect for such a situation. Standing at the doorway, Ms. Hernandez announces in a soft voice to each group of five or six students as they enter, "Go directly to your desk and follow the directions on the card that you will find there." When the students pick up their cards, they are busy reading and computing, and because they are curious about what they are to do, there is little off-task behavior. Because the teacher is not busy trying to provide directions to the entire class at once, she is able to circulate among the students, nipping discipline problems before they start.

Six minutes after the students began entering the room, all are working on the lesson with their partners. A few started working after only three minutes because they did not have to wait for directions. Significantly, the time that Ms. Hernandez's students spent obtaining directions and starting the planned lesson involved them in practice in computation and reading, and in acquiring a curiosity about the upcoming activity. (16)

Mr. Grah's students exhibited off-task behaviors while waiting for other students to enter the room and move to their places, while waiting for the teacher's directions, while jockeying for partners, and while waiting for materials to be distributed. Ms. Hernandez's students did not have to waste time doing any of these things. By thoroughly preparing for her lesson, Ms. Hernandez used her students' time more efficiently and gave students much less opportunity to be off task than did Mr. Grah.

Students with idle time on their hands are more likely to be disruptive than those who are busy (29). There are approximately 525,600 minutes in a year. For a 40-year-old teacher, each minute represents $1/21,024,000$ or 0.000000048 of that teacher's lifetime. But for a 13-year-old student, each minute represents $1/6,832,800$ or 0.000000146 of that student's lifetime. Thus the student perceives each minute to be approximately three times longer than does the teacher. The younger the person, the longer each moment seems to last.

Time is perceived to pass more slowly when a person is idle than when busy (32). Thus, when a student spends time idly waiting for the busy teacher, what seems to be a brief wait to the older person can seem an eternity to the younger one. Students tend to entertain themselves during these "eternities" by becoming disruptive.

You can plan lessons to minimize the time students spend receiving directions and getting started. Your preparation can also serve to free you from the burden of "running the show" during many lessons. When you are not lecturing, for example, you can be free to supervise and take care of any incidents of off-task behavior as they arise. In addition, planning a lesson so that it runs itself allows you to deal with the problem of one person without disrupting all students.

Here are some suggestions for planning lessons so that students' time is used efficiently.

1. Prepare visual displays prior to class meetings.

Do you ever spend class time with your back to students, writing on a chalkboard? If you do, try to limit this use of your students' time to making very brief notes that confine you to the board only momentarily. Whenever you need to present visual material, consider preparing it ahead of time. You can save much student time and be much more attentive to your class if you instantaneously display prepared material on an overhead transparency instead of writing on a chalkboard during class time.

2. Occasionally, direct students into lessons using handouts and modes other than oral presentations to the whole group.

In the initial anecdote of this chapter, Mr. Grah attempted to start his students on a planned lesson by giving the whole group verbal instructions. Those students who were ready to listen to the teacher sooner than others had to wait for everyone to settle down before they received the directions. In the second anecdote, Ms. Hernandez wrote out her instructions for the lesson in advance on cards and inside envelopes for each student to read. Not needing to tell everyone what to do at the same time afforded her the opportunity to move about the room to help, prod, or encourage those who needed it.

You can often avoid hassles and off-task student behaviors by using handouts and modes other than oral presentations to the whole group to communicate directions. Sometimes these alternatives are not practical, but when the lesson directions are complex or individualized and students can read, Ms. Hernandez's approach is usually more time-efficient than Mr. Grah's.

3. Sometimes prepare and distribute materials before students arrive in class.

Distributing materials ahead of time can be highly efficient, as it was for Ms. Hernandez. However, materials that are in the possession (or

16

even sight) of students before they are needed can be quite distracting. Sealed envelopes or some other type of container can keep materials out of sight and may even heighten students' curiosity about upcoming lessons.

4. **Use intraclass grouping to reduce student time spent waiting turns to be involved in lessons.**

Here are two contrasting examples that illustrate this suggestion:

Coach Caferell is drilling 13 baseball players on fielding ground balls. The players form a single line. The coach, standing some 70 feet away, throws a ground ball to the first player in line who attempts to scoop up the ball and throw it back to the coach. During this exercise, Coach Caferell provides words of encouragement and advice on techniques. Then the player goes to the end of the line to await another turn.

Coach Bergeron is drilling 13 baseball players on fielding ground balls. The players are divided into five groups of two and one group of three. Each group has a ball and the partners take turns either throwing ground balls or fielding them. Coach Bergeron circulates among the groups providing encouragement and advice on techniques.

Coach Caferell did not keep his players involved in the lesson; his players spent more time waiting in line than they spent practicing and learning. Because of his use of grouping, Coach Bergeron's students did more work in a shorter amount of time.

5. **Once you decide to use a grouping arrangement for a lesson, carefully devise a plan for getting students into the groups.**

If you decide to use a certain kind of intraclass grouping for a lesson, you must design a method for students to find their particular subgroups. The way you handle such a seemingly simple task can mean the difference between efficient grouping and the loss of valuable learning time.

You can decide (as did Mr. Grah) to have students determine their own grouping. Such an approach seems democratic enough and for many situations it is highly appropriate. However, it may result in the time-wasting behaviors that Mr. Grah's students exhibited. While necessary for some situations, student selection of their own groups opens up the potential for arguing and jockeying and may also lead to injured feelings when some individuals are excluded from a group. Obviously, this democratic option is not available when you wish to place certain students together and keep others apart.

Following are examples of two teachers controlling subgroup composition. In the first situation, the teacher's very businesslike approach leads to rapid student engagement. In the second, the teacher's use of a learning game facilitates group placement.

Ms. Maggio greets each member of her science class at the door of the classroom with a sheet of directions indicating where to go and what to do with whom. According to the directions, several subgroups are to perform experiments at specified stations around the room. Some minor disruptive complaints and some expressions of delight over the assignments are heard as the students move toward their stations. Two students unsuccessfully attempt to engage the teacher in an argument about her group choices for them.

Mr. Lambert wants his 33 history students to engage in a lesson in which they work in groups of threes. Prior to the lesson, he prepares 33 index cards. In one set, each of 11 cards contains the name of a different former U.S. president; in a second set, each of 11 cards contains the inauguration date of one of these presidents; and in a third set, each of 11 cards contains the name of the state in which one of these presidents was born. As the lesson is about to begin, Mr. Lambert hands each student a card. He does not care to control the exact composition of each subgroup during the lesson, but he wants to keep certain students apart. To do this, he gives each two students to be separated either two "president cards," two "date cards," or two "state cards." Then he instructs them to find their partners by locating the pair of cards that matches their own. Mr. Lambert's room is equipped with numerous reference books in which students are able to locate the necessary information. Thus, the time students spend locating their partners they also spend using reference books and discussing the content of the lesson.

---

6. Dispense with classroom administrative duties as efficiently and quickly as possible.

On numerous occasions, I have observed teachers spending 20 minutes of a 55-minute period taking roll, obtaining a lunch count, checking homework, collecting admit slips, and dealing with other administrative

18

matters. These delays not only waste class time, they also distract students from the real business of learning and make it more difficult for them to get on task when the time for a lesson finally arrives. Streamlining administrative chores can save a great deal of learning time. For example, once you know your students, you can determine who is present while checking homework or you can quickly count heads while students are busy with the lesson. Prepared forms with students' names and blocks for checking attendance, lunch status, homework status, and so on can also help you to dispense with record keeping and other routine matters with minimal infringement on class time.

TEACHER MOBILITY
AND CLASSROOM ARRANGEMENT

Is one of your students more likely to be off task when you are nearby or when you are across the room? Research findings suggest that you and your students are indeed unusual if you answered "nearby" (60). Compare the lesson styles of Ms. Stuckley and Mr. Coleman in the following anecdotes.

While conducting a grammar lesson for a class of 32 ninth graders, Ms. Stuckley stands by the chalkboard at the front of her classroom. She reads aloud from the textbook she holds in her hands and highlights salient points from the reading by listing them on the chalkboard. The students sit in their seats. They have been directed to follow the reading in their books, and to attend to Ms. Stuckley's comments and to her notes on the board.

Ms. Stuckley shifts her eyes from the book, to the students, to the chalkboard, and the lesson continues. Some students read along and are quite attentive, especially those sitting in the front row. The attention of other students, especially those near the rear of the room, occasionally drifts from the lesson. Because their attention lapses a few times, some students do not follow the last part of the lesson and begin to lose interest.

While conducting a grammar lesson for his ninth graders, Mr. Coleman circulates among his 32 students. He reads from the textbooks of various students over their shoulders and makes comments. He has appointed one student to stand in front of the class with a textbook to record notes on the chalkboard as he highlights salient points from the reading.

When Mr. Coleman notices a student's attention drifting away from the lesson, he moves toward the student, finds his place in the student's book with a finger or simply puts a hand on the student's shoulder, and reads.

Plan to conduct your classes (as Mr. Coleman did) so that you can move about the room without disrupting the lesson. This suggestion will be easier to follow if your classroom is arranged so that you can easily move between any points in the room. Questions concerning optimum classroom size and ideal room shape have been studied extensively (54). Unfortunately, most teachers have had little or nothing to say about either the design or the size of their classrooms. Therefore they must make the most of the situation by careful and creative room arrangement. One way to do this is to break out of the traditional rectangular array of desks and modify the arrangement so that you can be within physical reach of any student as fast as you can walk across the room.

Chapter 3
SECURING
STUDENTS' INTEREST

> There is a space between man's imagination
> and man's attainment that may only be tra-
> versed by his longing.
>
> —Kahlil Gibran, *Sand and Foam*

PROBLEM-SOLVING LESSONS

It is important that teachers realize that students often fail to remain engaged in lessons because they find the activities to be either boring or irrelevant to their concerns (30). It may not be possible to deny students their perceptions. But it is possible to modify at least some of the lessons, to make them more interesting to students, and to make them address student concerns more directly. I do not suggest that lessons should be "fun and games." On the contrary, lessons are serious business.

First of all, examine the goals and objectives of your lessons and determine how, if at all, your students will benefit from accomplishing each goal. When I examined the goals of my lessons, I found that they fell into four categories:

1. Goals that address my students' needs which they perceive as important.

2. Goals that address my students' needs but which they do not perceive as important.

3. Goals that do not address my students' needs but for which I am held responsible by supervisors for helping students attain.

4. Goals that do not address my students' needs for which I am not held responsible by supervisors for helping students attain.

I have little difficulty developing lessons that produce high levels of student engagement when those lessons have goals that fall in the first category. I will not, however, get students engaged in lessons with goals in the second category unless I design mechanisms into those lessons that help students discover for themselves that the goals are indeed something important for them to accomplish. I have never been very successful in telling students how important something is, but I have been highly successful (as have many other teachers) in getting students to realize the importance of a lesson by using a problem-solving approach (7). Two contrasting anecdotes illustrate this approach. The first involves a history unit designed to help students accomplish a goal in a traditional manner. The second involves a history unit using a problem-solving approach to help students accomplish the same goal.

Mr. Remigus designs a two-week unit to help his high school history class accomplish the following learning goal: "Students will better understand the workings of the U.S. Congress between 1901 and 1935." The unit consists of the following learning activities:

1. Mr. Remigus lectures on the importance of understanding the workings of Congress during the era to be studied.
2. The class is assigned to read a chapter in a textbook and to answer the corresponding questions in the supplemental workbook.
3. Mr. Remigus reviews answers to workbook questions with the class.
4. Students are assigned special topics (e.g., the fight for women's suffrage and the Prohibition Act) on which they are to complete library papers.

Ms. Boeker designs a two-week unit to help her high school history class accomplish the following learning goal: "Students will better understand the workings of the U.S. Congress between 1901 and 1935." Ms. Boeker makes a number of observations of her students in order to identify current issues that concern them. She decides to focus on the following problems:

1. Should marijuana be legalized?
2. What should the federal government do about unemployment?

3. What should Congress do to ensure the rights of ethnic minorities?

4. Does the United States need an Equal Rights Amendment?

5. What should the federal government do about abortions?

6. What stand should the federal government take on combating pollution?

Ms. Boeker decides to build the learning activities of her two-week unit around these six current problems. When her plan is implemented, the lesson follows this course:

1. Ms. Boeker assigns each class member to one of six task groups (according to her perceptions of student interests and her choice of student groups). One group, consisting of six students, is directed to "research" the first problem, concerning the legalization of marijuana. These students are to examine how Congress handled the prohibition of alcohol in the first 30 years of the twentieth century and then relate those "lessons of history" to the current question of marijuana. Specifically, the group is directed to explain Congress's rationale for repealing prohibition, including the benefits and consequences of the repeal, and to identify both similarities and differences between the question of alcohol prohibition in the earlier era and marijuana prohibition today. Each of the other five task groups, consisting of about six students each, researches one of the other five problems in the same manner.

2. Ms. Boeker provides each task group with an organizational structure within which to operate, a list of resources from which to acquire information, a list of deadlines for specific subtasks, and an indication of how to report findings to the rest of the class and to the teacher.

3. In order to obtain an overall picture of the climate within which the Congress operated from 1901 to 1935, and thus to be better able to compare the problems of that time with those of the present, each student is directed to read a textbook chapter dealing with the years from 1901 to 1935.

4. Each task group receives a schedule for making periodic progress reports to the entire class.

5. After each task group presents its final report to the class, a brief meeting is held for all class members who were not part of the reporting group, with members of the reporting group

acting as observers. At the meeting, students consider and vote upon the task group proposals that relate to the current problem.

Which of the two units do you think better held the students' interest? Mr. Remigus attempted to get his students to recognize the value of their activity by telling them about the value. But telling is not teaching. Ms. Boeker's plan focused her students' attention on problems that were very real to them, which they had a desire to solve. Her lessons did not divorce history from students' current concerns. As a result, their learning served a very real purpose in the minds of her students. The teacher did not have to tell the students how important the lesson was because its importance became apparent to them.

It is, of course, virtually impossible to develop a lesson focusing on students' concerns if the goal does not address students' needs (that is, if it is a goal in the third or fourth category described earlier). Goals that do not address students' needs should be eliminated from the curriculum. If supervisors expect you to teach to such goals, then you may need to use a fun-and-games approach to maintain student engagement until you are able to convince the supervisors that the goals are inappropriate.

INVOLVING ALL STUDENTS
IN LESSONS

Do you use questioning strategies in your lessons? Learning theory suggests that you should (47, 79) and research suggests that you are typical if you do (62). The following is an example of a questioning strategy session that I observed:

Ms. Ling uses an overhead projector to display six sequences to 29 mathematics students. She asks, "What do you see?" Willie: "Some numbers." Ms. Ling: "Anything special about all six sets of numbers?" Anna Mae: "There is an order." Ms. Ling: "What's an ordered set called?" Anna Mae: "A sequence!" Nettie: "Or a vector." Ms. Ling: "So we have six sequences of vectors...What else do you notice?...Okay, Willie?" Willie: "Three of them are written in blue and the rest in red. Why is that?" Woodrow: "Because she used different pens, you..." Ms. Ling (interrupting Woodrow): "The sequences in red are special. They belong together for a reason other than that I

24

used the same pen to write them out." "I know!" shouts Ory, raising his hand. Ms. Ling: "Okay?" Ory: "The blue numbers are all perfect squares!" Nettie: "No, 90 isn't a perfect square!" Ms. Ling: "Anna Mae, thanks for raising your hand. What do you think?" Anna Mae: "All the members of any red sequence have a common factor."

Ms. Ling's inductive questioning strategy session leading to the discovery of geometric sequences continues.

What is your opinion of this brief glimpse of Ms. Ling's lesson? I am impressed with her approach to helping students conceptualize. However, I am concerned that only several of the 29 students appeared involved in the session. Like most teachers, Ms. Ling provided very little time between each of her questions and each student's answer (4). Only students who were quick to respond and outspoken like Anna Mae and Willie became engaged in the lesson. Imagine some ways that Ms. Ling could have conducted this session so that all the students formulated their own answers to each question. After all, students hardly benefit from this type of questioning strategy session unless they attempt to develop their own answers. Here are three possible alternatives that Ms. Ling might consider:

1. She might frame questions with directions similar to these: "I am going to ask a question. Each of you is to answer the question in your mind. Don't tell us your answer or volunteer to do so until I call on you. Just silently hold your answer in your mind . . . Okay, how do the sequences written in red differ from those written in blue?" Ms. Ling should then provide time for all students to think of something. She might prompt students with, "Eddie, have you thought of your answer yet?" Eddie: "Yes, ma'am." Ms. Ling: "Fine, hang on to it. How about you, Judy?" . . . If students volunteer or speak out before the class is ready, Ms. Ling should focus attention away from them. After all, the thinking of a student who is trying to develop an answer will be disrupted upon hearing a classmate's answer. Ms. Ling might terminate the wait with, "Maunsell, give us your answer." Maunsell responds . . . Ms. Ling: "How about yours, Mary?" Mary responds . . . Ms. Ling: "Danny, compare Mary's answer with Maunsell's."

2. Another possibility is for Ms. Ling to require each student to write answers to questions on a sheet of paper. She could then circulate throughout the room, quietly reading answers while looking over

25

students' shoulders. After everyone has written something, she should select students to read answers aloud. In this way, she would not only involve more students, but she would also have the answers that would be most beneficial to the discussion read aloud.

3. Ms. Ling might also consider having students formulate answers in subgroups and then have the groups report their answers to the whole class for discussion.

Any of these suggestions should engage more students in developing their own answers to the questions.

Students often become disinterested in a lesson because the pace is either too slow or too fast for them. For example, they may have already achieved the lesson's goal, or they may lack prerequisites for achieving the goal. Even classes that are homogeneously grouped according to ability can contain several achievement levels so that the problem persists (80). Flexible within-class groups can sometimes help maintain the interest of a class composed of a wide range of achievement levels. Here is an example:

Mr. Citerelli is a secondary school English teacher who uses informal observations and formal tests to preassess his students' abilities, not only for the objectives that he helps them achieve, but also for prerequisite skills such as reading levels. In addition, he conducts surveys of student interests and assesses student attitudes toward learning. Then he uses this information to design lessons that incorporate a variety of within-class grouping patterns.

During one lesson Mr. Citerelli is attempting to help tenth graders improve their writing talents. Students are to work in pairs, gathering information on a topic, and then presenting a written report on the topic to the remainder of the class. From his prior observations and preassessments, Mr. Citerelli knows that Gomez displays advanced writing skills while Simon lacks both interest and skill in writing. The teacher realizes, however, that Simon is very interested in interscholastic wrestling while Gomez shows no interest in such sports. Mr. Citerelli decides to group Simon and Gomez together for the writing assignment and require them to report on the various area high school wrestling teams. He believes that this design will allow each boy's strengths to complement the other. Simon will learn about writing from Gomez, while Gomez will depend upon Simon's knowledge and interest in wrestling to complete the report. Such grouping, the teacher thinks, will require Gomez to practice advanced writing skills since he will have to apply his writing talents to an unfamiliar subject. The teacher also believes that in time Simon will increase his interest in writing because of his interest in the topic and because he will be depended upon to provide the necessary expertise for the writing assignment.

Teachers sometimes view the diversity of interests and achievement levels existing among their students as a hindrance to a smoothly operating classroom. But one way to take advantage of this diversity is to use *flexible* within-class or intraclass grouping, as Mr. Citerelli did.

Chapter 4

ESTABLISHING
RULES OF CONDUCT

Insecurity is endemic to the beginning teacher. She wants assurance. As a result, some
teachers seek to be popular with their students.
There is a difference between popularity and a
genuine helping relationship.

—Kevin Ryan and James Cooper,
Those Who Can, Teach

PURPOSES OF RULES

Like most teachers at King High School, Ms. Loberg has a rule prohibiting students from wearing hats in the classroom. Ms. Loberg grew
up with the notion that hats are not to be worn indoors and that boys
and men display poor taste by doing so. Ms. Loberg frequently finds
herself interrupting her lessons to deal with a hat-wearing student. She
is especially nervous about violation of this rule because occasionally
Coach Krause, a colleague who tries to "help out" inexperienced
women teachers such as Ms. Loberg, has come into her classroom
and pulled a student from his seat for wearing a hat. Ms. Loberg is flat-
tered by Coach Krause's attention, so she does not tell him to discontinue this "help." However, she is annoyed by his disruptive
interference.

Rules should be established to serve only one or more of the following
purposes:

28

1. *To Maximize On-Task Behaviors*. Rules that protect students from disruptions during lessons are necessary. Normally, the wearing of hats during a lesson is not disruptive.

2. *To Discourage Disruptions to Other Classes or Persons Located in or Near the School*. Even on-task behaviors of one group of students during a lesson can disturb another group during a different lesson. For example, music students in one room who are singing loudly may be on task, but at the same time they may be distracting students in an adjoining room who are viewing a film. The school community should be protected from such disturbances. Ms. Loberg's prohibition against wearing hats did not serve this purpose.

3. *To Provide a Safe, Secure Environment for Students, School Personnel, and Visitors to the School Campus*. A school can hardly function if its campus is unsafe. Hat wearing rarely poses a threat to safety.

4. *To Maintain Acceptable Standards of Decorum Among Students, School Personnel, and Visitors to the School*. If Ms. Loberg's rule prohibiting hats could be justified, it would be based on this fourth purpose. A school community operates more effectively when common courtesy is practiced by all. However, teachers or other school personnel with governing responsibilities should not attempt to remake students in their own image. Ms. Loberg may have thought wearing a hat in a classroom displayed poor taste, but obviously hat-wearing students did not find the practice distasteful. When rules of courtesy are being established for a heterogeneous mix of students from a variety of backgrounds, it is advisable to define discourtesy in terms of what inconveniences others and not simply in terms of what one cultural group considers unbecoming.

An unnecessary rule—one that does not serve any of these four purposes—creates problems for teachers. Once a rule is established, teachers become responsible for its enforcement. Unenforced rules serve to teach students that rules in general need not be taken seriously. The existence of unnecessary rules undesirably affects individual students in one or more of the following ways:

1. Students who heed unnecessary rules become conditioned to being regulated by authority even when there is no rational basis for such regulation.

29

2. Students who resist unnecessary rules "get into trouble"; this disturbs their on-task behaviors and usually "turns them off" to school.

3. Students tend to generalize that if some rules are unimportant, then other rules are also unimportant.

DETERMINING RULES

Whatever rules are determined, each regulation should be justified in terms of one or more of the four purposes stated. Ideally, classroom rules should correspond to general systemwide and schoolwide policies and regulations—such as a schoolwide policy regulating food consumption on school property. In many schools, however, inconsistency exists between the rules established for different classrooms (15). Such inconsistency is especially confusing to students who are governed by two or more sets of conflicting rules in a departmentalized school. For example, a student may be allowed to borrow from classmates in a math class, but not in a Spanish language class.

When to establish rules for an individual classroom is a question that causes controversy among educators. Jacobsen suggests that a teacher should see that classroom rules are established at the outset of the school year (44). This view cites the advantages of preventing disruptions by immediately regulating procedures for speaking, moving about, obtaining materials, and other recurring matters. Other educators agree with Brown's position that the disadvantages of immediately setting rules usually outweigh the advantages:

> Establishing a rigid set of standards at the outset potentially raises two additional problems. First, the rules established by the teacher may prescribe behavior for students who have been previously reinforced for breaking rules; and secondly, it places the teacher in the position of enforcing rules which although made to do so, do not fit all students in all situations. For these reasons, it seems to be unwise strategy to establish a large number of rules at the outset.
>
> When, then, should rules be set forth? Simply, when the need for a rule arises. Because most students have learned that groups have rules, many of them will ask during the first meeting about classroom regulations. Since the request comes from students, the teacher is in an excellent position to launch into a democratic approach to classroom discipline. At this point, students can be asked about rules which

are needed for optimal learning. Some preliminary rules are then established with students. Additional rules can be established when the need for them arises. Rules are needed whenever the behavior of students endangers the attainment of class goals or when the rights of others, including the teacher, are infringed upon. (14)

No matter when they are established, there is general agreement that a few clearly stated classroom rules that encompass a broad range of situations are far more effective than a long list of regulations, each one of which deals with a specific situation. Brophy and Putnam recommend that rules be stated in functional terms rather than in restrictive, absolute terms (11). For example, "When you finish individual classwork before others, be careful not to disturb students who are still working" is preferable to "Remain silently in your seat after completing classwork until the teacher tells you that you may talk and move about."

Ms. Cheek has a rule in her seventh grade class that during any group test, each student should turn in his/her paper upon completing it and then return silently to his/her seat and sit there until all test papers have been turned in to the teacher.

During one such test, Malcolm and Lorenzo have both completed their tests and are waiting for others to finish. Kim is sitting at the desk between the two boys, still taking her test, when Malcolm raises himself out of his seat to lean over Kim to hand Lorenzo a pencil. Upon observing this disturbance, Ms. Cheek beckons Malcolm to her, saying, "Do you know the rule about getting out of your seat?" Malcolm: "Yes, but I was only giving Lorenzo his pencil. I didn't get out of my seat." Ms. Cheek: "How could you return Lorenzo's pencil to him and remain in your seat?" Malcolm: "My left knee never left my seat, I stretched way over." Ms. Cheek: "Well, that's getting out of your seat!" Malcolm: "Even if my knee was still touching?"

This inane conversation and ridiculous waste of time could have been avoided if Ms. Cheek's rule had been stated in functional terms rather than in restrictive, absolute terms. The real concern should not have been whether Malcolm left his seat, but whether he was disturbing other students who were still taking the test. Ms. Cheek's regulation did not seem to be directed consistently toward the prevention of disturbances. During the test while classmates were still working, students were permitted to walk up to the teacher's desk when ready to turn in their papers and when beckoned by the teacher. This defeated the purpose of avoiding disturbances by remaining in one's seat.

If Ms. Cheek's rule were stated in such terms as "Be careful not to disturb classmates who are still taking their tests," judgment could be exercised in specific situations as to what were reasonable ways of preventing disturbances. Without technically leaving his seat (according to his interpretation), Malcolm disturbed his classmates who were taking the test. Whether or not he left his seat was unimportant. But he should learn to care about protecting classmates' opportunities to take tests.

Teachers have the responsibility for seeing that necessary classroom rules are established. However, do these rules serve their four purposes more effectively when teachers determine them or when the students themselves agree upon them? In other words, should you use authoritarian means to determine regulations, should you determine them yourself but base them upon student input, or should your students determine them democratically? Provided that you determine them shrewdly, there are advantages to establishing classroom rules without benefit of student discussion or input. When adequate reflection and flexibility are employed, such authoritarian tactics can be time-efficient and effective. Students who are never given the opportunity to question regulations openly and exert an influence on their determination may be more inclined to follow them without expressing opposition. On the other hand, once an issue is open for class discussion, students who disagree with its resolution tend to continue to discuss it even after it has been decided upon. That is, students who voted against a rule adopted by the majority may not accept it without at least verbal opposition.

You may choose to retain the right to make the rules, but allow your determination to be influenced by student opinions. The following anecdote gives an example of this practice.

Ms. Clifford tells her class, "I have received three separate complaints that other classes were disturbed while some of us were going to the library. We will continue to need to make trips to the library during this period for the next three or four weeks. Should a rule be made to prevent any of us from disturbing other classes?" A number of students raise their hands. Ms. Clifford: "Dale?" Dale: "The trouble is that three or four of us go at once. Maybe you should allow only one to go at a time." Ms. Clifford: "I will consider that. Any other suggestions?...Jim?" Jim: "Find out who's causing trouble and don't let them go to the library again. They can do their assignments after school." Yolanda: "But we really weren't doing anything wrong!...Mrs. Crooks is always trying to get us in trouble." Ms. Clifford: "That's irrelevant, Yolanda. I really don't care about what has already happened. I just want to make sure that we don't disturb other classes in the future." Jean: "Do we really need a rule if we just promise to keep quiet from now on?" Ms. Clifford: "That's what I would like to decide... How many of you think that we need a rule to cover this situation? Raise your hands... One, two, three... Mmmm, most of you believe we need a rule... Okay, let's not take much more time with this now. I would like each of you to take out a sheet of paper and suggest what you think I should do in one to three sentences. Please do not put your name on the paper... I'll take your papers home with me and consider your suggestions tonight. I'll have a decision for you in the morning."

Ms. Clifford's method for determining this rule provided her with the benefit of the group's collective wisdom. While she retained her right to decide upon the rule, she elicited her students' opinions in a manner that did not waste time with irrelevant discussions. If she uses their suggestions at times and explains her decisions whenever she does not, the students are more likely to understand and cooperate with the rules than in cases where teachers are more authoritarian.

Many would agree that in a society that values democracy, the concept is best learned by students when they govern themselves democratically. Furthermore, it can be argued that students are more likely to appreciate and adhere to regulations that are established by their own vote. Under such a system of rule making, the teacher's role is threefold:

1. To establish the necessary structure for democratic determination of the rules

2. To provide leadership to encourage the establishment of appropriate rules

3. To ensure that democratic processes are followed so that each student has the opportunity to participate.

Mr. Cooper has 12 hand-held, battery-operated calculators available in his classroom for the use of his 32 eighth graders. The calculators are kept in a box on a supply table in the back of the room. Except for certain exercises designed to improve students' computational skills and certain tests designed to assess those computational skills, students generally have free access to the calculators.

In time, however, Mr. Cooper notices with increasing frequency that calculators are left on when not in use and that students fail to return them quickly to the box after use. Also, students begin to complain that they have trouble obtaining a working calculator when they need one. The teacher maintains a supply of batteries purchased with class treasury money. Funds for the treasury were supplied by class moneymaking projects and by monies paid by students for materials, such as pencils.

Mr. Cooper calls a "class community meeting" to address complaints about the calculators. Whenever these meetings are held, the students know that they are operating under *Robert's Rules of Order* (64) and they can raise issues of common concern. At this meeting, Mr. Cooper describes the recurring problems of calculator use; he proposes that the situation be resolved.

After a discussion, the group agrees that rules governing the use of the calculators are needed. A motion made by Roy and seconded by another student states that anyone who does not turn a calculator off and return it to the supply table will never again be allowed to use one. After some discussion, the motion is amended to change the restriction of calculator use by offending students from life to a week for the first offense, two weeks for the second, and so forth. Mr. Cooper and several students argue that the motion should be voted down for now and other proposals considered that would take care of the problem without restricting calculator use. They base their argument on two points:

1. Students' work would be impaired if the calculators were not available to them.

2. Such a rule would at times place the class or the teacher in the undesirable position of having to determine who left a calculator on or who failed to return one.

The motion fails 14 to 15 with two abstentions and one student absent. Amanda then proposes that students be allowed to use calculators only while standing at the supply table. She argues that they should be able to use them without removing them from the area, that the machines might be secured to the table. The motion is defeated after students argue that the table would become congested and they need the calculators at their desks. After further discussion the following motion finally passes:

The batteries will be removed from the calculators and those batteries will be held in storage. Four unused batteries will be distributed to each student from those already in storage and from additional ones purchased from the class treasury. (Each calculator takes four AA batteries to operate.)

Each calculator will be marked with an identification numeral

34

and kept in the supply table box without batteries. Each student may obtain a calculator by checking it out, writing his/her name, time, and date, and the calculator's numeral on a check-out/check-in sheet to be left on the supply table. While using a calculator, students are to use their own batteries, which they are to remove before returning the equipment to the box.

Students will be required to maintain their own supply of batteries just as they do their pencils and paper. Batteries will be kept on hand for sale when needed, at a profit for the class treasury.

The motion seems a bit complicated, but Mr. Cooper helps students work out the necessary procedural details that make the written rule appear complex. Once the regulation is in effect for a week or so, however, it leads to established behavior patterns that students follow with little thought of the written description in the minutes of the class community meetings.

COMMUNICATING RULES TO STUDENTS

To be effective, classroom rules must be understood by class members. Students will not always grasp the meaning and intent of rules that have been related to them. Just as students understand and misunderstand subject matter content in varying degrees, so too do they understand and interpret rules differently. Thus, it is necessary to teach the significance, intent, meaning, and consequences of classroom regulations. For most rules, especially with older students, the lessons may simply involve displaying and discussing them with an ongoing use of appropriate cues. For more complex rules, more elaborate lessons may be necessary, especially with younger students. Gudmundsen suggests that students participate in role-playing sessions to demonstrate rules (40). In the following example, Ms. Joseph used role playing to help her sixth graders understand two rules.

Ms. Joseph announces to her class: "Adella, Kayleen, and Craig have been rehearsing a skit for you. Adella will play the role of the teacher, while Kayleen and Craig will act as two students during a class discussion. Although we have only three actors on our 'stage,' keep in mind that Kayleen and Craig are just two of a whole class of students. Imagine them surrounded by others . . . After the skit, we will discuss what we heard and saw . . . Okay, take over, actors."

Adella: Would anyone in the class like to tell us his or her fa-

35

vorite historical character from those we've studied so far this year? (Kayleen raises her hand.) Yes, Kayleen.

Kayleen: I don't know if he's my favorite, but I really like Gandhi.

Adella: Tell us why Gandhi appeals to you.

Kayleen: Because he was able to accept people of—

Craig (Interrupting): George Washington, he's the father of our country! I like George!

Kayleen: Nobody cares what you think or like!

At this point Ms. Joseph says, "Okay, that's the end of our skit." Then she conducts a discussion in which class members empathize with the characters, and she points out how Craig violated the class rule: "Allow others the freedom to speak during class discussions." The consequences of Craig's interruption are also brought out, as are the consequences of Kayleen's violation of another rule: "Be considerate of the feelings of others."

ENFORCING RULES

An existing rule that is not enforced or that is inconsistently enforced is far more detrimental to the smooth operation of a class than one that has never been established. Students need to be able to predict the consequences of their actions.

Chapter 5

AVOIDING MISCOMMUNICATION

Should you really open your eyes and see,
you would behold your image in all images,
    And should you open your ears and listen,
you would hear your own voice in all voices.

—Kahlil Gibran, *Sand and Foam*

AVOID BEING OFF TASK YOURSELF

Do you remember having a lesson interrupted by another adult—a principal, a parent, a teacher, or a supervisor—who, after apologizing, asked to speak with you? How did you react to the situation? Did you apologize to your students and then speak with the individual? If so, what impression did this make on your students? By allowing an avoidable interruption in a lesson to occur, you unwittingly communicate to your students that the lesson is of secondary importance. By quickly apologizing to the adult and asking to speak after the lesson, you communicate to your students that the lesson is important to you. Once teachers get off task, it is difficult for students to become reengaged when teachers are ready to resume the lesson. Students will model their teachers' behavior (53). Unless teachers display a business-like attitude toward lessons, they cannot expect their students to take their work seriously.

Do not be disruptive yourself. Compare the two anecdotes that fol-

37

low. In one, the teacher creates a more serious disruption than the one she is handling.

Ms. Blythe is lecturing to her eleventh grade class. Jane, one of her 26 students, begins tapping her pencil against her desk top and looking around. Ms. Blythe finds Jane's behavior annoying and judges it to be a potential distraction to other students. She interrupts her own lecture, turns to Jane from the front of the room, and complains, "Will you stop that noise? Can't you do what you're supposed to do?"

Ms. Guevarra is lecturing to her eleventh grade class. Jean, one of her 26 students, begins tapping her pencil against her desk top and looking around. Ms. Guevarra finds Jean's behavior annoying and judges it to be a potential distraction to the other students. She continues her lecture as she walks to a point near the girl. Jean stops looking around and attends to the lecture, but she keeps tapping her pencil. Ms. Guevarra gently removes the pencil from her hand. Jean receives the message. Other class members are unaware of what is happening as their attention is not disturbed by the teacher's handling of the incident.

Ms. Blythe's response to Jane's off-task behavior appeared to be a reaction to annoyance that resulted in an attack on Jane's personality. Instead of focusing her attention on the problem of reengaging Jane in the lesson, she interrupted the lesson with an irrelevant, rhetorical question ("Can't you do what you're supposed to do?"). Such tactics may have succeeded in getting Jane to stop tapping and looking around. However, they not only interrupted the other students, but they did not engage Jane in the lesson. Jane was too busy pondering the incident, which she probably found insulting and embarrassing, and only pretended to be attending to the lecture. She would be a very unusual teenager if she were able to concentrate on the content of the lecture immediately after being asked in front of her peers, "Can't you do what you're supposed to do?"

AVOID SENDING UNINTENDED MESSAGES

Students in Ms. Coco's French language class are exempted from weekend homework assignments if they have a "perfect conduct" record for the week. Those who have "misbehaved" during the week are assigned weekend homework.

Ms. Coco was unwittingly teaching students that homework assignments are a punishment and no homework assignments are a reward. If such assignments help students achieve worthwhile goals, then doing them certainly must be important to all students. It may appear strange, but a more logical course for Ms. Coco to follow would be to reward "perfect conduct" by assigning homework and to punish "misbehavior" by not assigning it. This logic is, of course, nonsense, however, but only if homework assignments are intended to help all students achieve worthwhile learning goals.

Ms. Criss "catches" Quinn, one of her tenth graders, shooting paperclips across her room. She sends him to an assistant principal who administers three swats to Quinn's buttocks with a wooden paddle.

Shooting paperclips is a dangerous practice that no teacher should tolerate. But what did Ms. Criss and the assistant principal unwittingly teach Quinn by their actions? They intended to teach him not to shoot paperclips in the classroom. However, research suggests that the experience did not teach the boy that lesson (27). Besides a possible lesson about getting caught, Quinn may have learned that one human being hitting another is perfectly acceptable behavior condoned by school authorities. Quinn may model the assistant principal's actions and develop a pattern of punishing others by inflicting pain (34). The undesirable effects of corporal punishment are well documented (43).

Because they are continually dealing with highly complex and impressionable human beings, it is important that teachers pause and reflect on the consequences of their words and actions. By doing so, they can avoid unknowingly creating additional problems when they attempt to deal with a particular incident.

AVOID TEACHING STUDENTS TO IGNORE YOU

Unfortunately, many students readily learn to be "deaf" to teachers because of exposure to meaningless conversations with adults. Note the following example:

Rutherford is working in a small reading group in Ms. Sorenson's sixth grade class when he gets up and begins walking across the room. Ms. Sorenson sees him and says, "Rutherford, don't get up!"

By the time Ms. Sorenson told Rutherford not to get up, he was already up and walking. It was possible for Rutherford to sit down, but it was impossible for him never to have stood up once he did so. Ms. Sorenson was unwittingly teaching him not to listen to her by giving a direction that he could not possibly obey. It was too late to tell him not to get up. Possibly, she should have told him to return to his place and sit down. Generally speaking, instead of an immediate verbal reaction to students' behavior, teachers should pause and carefully frame their words before speaking.

Adults often send pointless messages to children because they react to situations before they are aware of some pertinent circumstance. Here is an example:

Mr. Hickenlooper directs his tenth graders to read silently pages 78 through 81 at their desks. Noticing Kezia talking to Richard, he says, "Kezia, didn't I say 'silently'?" Kezia replies, "I'm sorry, but I was just telling him the page numbers." Mr. Hickenlooper: "Then that's okay."

Although exchanges such as this cannot always be avoided, they can in time become destructive if they occur habitually. Mr. Hickenlooper's behavior was surely not reprehensible. However, if Kezia were only giving Richard page numbers, the talking would have self-terminated without the teacher's intervention. By first waiting to see if the talking would quickly stop, the teacher could have avoided a useless exchange of words.

Sometimes teachers and other adults act as if they are terminating a self-terminating behavior or initiating a self-initiating behavior. In these instances they also teach students to ignore them. The following anecdote offers an example:

At Francis Parker High School teachers are expected to stand in their doorways between classes in order to enforce the hall rules, which include *no running.* Ms. Larsen is standing by her door when she sees Thelma and Emily running toward the room next door. Just as the girls reach their room, they hear Ms. Larsen yell, "Stop running!" At this time they are about to stop running, not because of Ms. Larsen's words, but because they have reached their destination.

While no real harm resulted from this incident, it would have been better if Ms. Larsen had either said and done nothing about the girls' running or intervened with some technique for preventing their running in the future. For example, she might have called to the girls before they reached their room to remind them about the rule. As it happened, Ms. Larsen's action served only to remind the students that teachers say some things that mean nothing to them. Thus students can learn to ignore teachers.

Another way that adults encourage students to ignore them is to make judgments for them. For example:

Ms. Boynton is introducing a social studies activity to her ninth graders. In the activity students will examine each other's political beliefs. She announces: "You're really going to like this! It's a lot of fun. It really gets exciting when . . ."

If Ms. Boynton continued in this vein, she would "turn off" her students. Whether or not the students would enjoy the activity, they would judge for themselves. Some would probably find it exciting; others would not. By getting on with the directions so that the students could become engaged in the activity, Ms. Boynton would let them find out for themselves just how much fun and how exciting the lesson was. If Ms. Boynton found the activity to be fun and exciting, she should quickly pass the information on to the students by telling them, "I found this very exciting; I hope you will also." The students would probably like to know how she feels. But she only wasted words by trying to inform them of their feelings. Students will decide their own feelings about the experience individually as they become involved in it. Teachers usually spend too much time trying to persuade students about the value of a lesson when they are uneasy about students' reception of the activity.

USE SUPPORTIVE REPLIES

Mr. Grey's eighth graders are working on a computational exercise when Lisa brings her worksheet to him and exclaims, "I just can't do these! They're too hard for me." Mr. Grey responds, "Aw, come on, Lisa, you can do them. They're not really difficult for a smart girl like you..."

Ms. Johnson's eighth graders are working on a computational exercise when Dennis brings his worksheet to her and exclaims, "I just can't do these! They're too hard for me." Ms. Johnson responds, "Dividing decimals can be very difficult. I see that you are having trouble..."

In situations of this kind, students' frustrations often need to be dealt with before the sources of their frustrations can be effectively addressed. Ms. Johnson's style of communication is *supportive*, whereas Mr. Grey's is *nonsupportive*. A response to an expression of frustration that sends the message "I hear and understand what you told me and it's okay to feel as you do" is considered supportive (65). Ms. Johnson was supportive because, before trying to help Dennis with the computations, she let him know that she understood what he told her. Mr. Grey, on the other hand, contradicted Lisa's statement. He was nonsupportive; he did not accept her feelings. He attempted to encourage Lisa by telling her she could do the work. This well-meaning comment only informed the girl that the teacher did not understand her dilemma. Obviously, the computations were difficult for her, yet Mr. Grey told her they were not difficult for a smart girl. Consequently Lisa understood from this remark that she was not smart. Mr. Grey's well-meaning, but nonsupportive, reply increased Lisa's frustration because she then perceived the additional problem of dealing with a teacher who lacked empathy.

AVOID LABELING STUDENTS

Many times I have stopped myself from making comments that label students—for example, "You're really smart, Jake!" or "Why are you so lazy, Ginnie?" Instead, I catch myself and say, "Jake, you really seem to understand why the quadratic formula works!" or "Ginnie, why did you waste so much time today?" Teachers need to make concerted efforts to address specifically the student's achievement or lack of achievement, behavior, or concern. They also need to avoid inferences that label or characterize students (75).

The fact that a student does not comprehend the messages from several readings does not necessarily imply that the student is a "slow learner" or even a "poor reader." It only means that he or she did not grasp the messages from those readings. The student's lack of comprehension might stem from a lack of interest in the material, from thought patterns that tend to diverge from those of the authors of the readings, or from a number of causes that do not fall under a general label such as "poor reader." Students who acquire a general label such as "poor reader" are, however, likely to find they have difficulty reading even when they are interested in the material, when they have no misconceptions about the content, and when they do not think divergently from the author.

By the same token, because a student readily comprehends what is generally considered a scientific concept that is difficult to grasp does not necessarily imply that the student is especially "bright" or even that the student has a "scientific mind." It only means that she or he grasps that particular scientific concept. To label such students "bright" or "scientific-minded" is to ask them to live up to someone else's image and to teach them to be elitist. Furthermore, to label such students "bright" is to unwittingly label those who do not grasp the concept "dull" (35).

That a student is disruptive during several or even many lessons does not imply hostility or a behavior problem. Students become disruptive because they are bored, they do not recognize value in being on task, they seek attention, or they feel defensive about participating in the lesson, or because of a number of other reasons that are not inherent in their personalities. Students who learn that they are thought of as "behavior problems" feel obliged to live with—or even up to—that label. They find themselves in a "no-win" situation because they believe the teacher does not care about them. They think, "Who wants to tolerate a behavior problem?" On the other hand, students who learn that they are "okay" (41), even though they display certain behaviors that are problems, may be willing to alter those behaviors.

Students would be much less defensive and consequently much more likely to cooperate if adults did not require them to put their self-worth on the line whenever they undertake a task or whenever they are expected to behave in a prescribed manner. Unfortunately, students often think their self-worth is in jeopardy whenever they attempt tasks prescribed by teachers. By avoiding miscommunication in the classroom, teachers can do much to prevent this student reaction.

Chapter 6

DEALING WITH
OFF-TASK BEHAVIORS

> It seems to me, that just as it usually seems to my kind, that society was simply trying to strip or rip my shield, that it was willing to do so ruthlessly, that it didn't care about me personally, or the amount of humiliation or degradation it might inflict in the process. I stubbornly balked at being manipulated, regulated, or being compelled to conform blindly through fear or threat of punishment, however severe. Instead, I came to question the validity of a society that appeared more concerned with imposing its will than in inspiring respect. There seemed to me something grossly wrong with this. "We'll make you be good!" I was told, and I told myself nobody should, would or could *make* me anything. And I proved it.
>
> —Caryl Chessman, *Cell 2455 Death Row*

USE A SYSTEMATIC APPROACH

By maintaining students' interest, effectively managing time and space, avoiding miscommunication, and effectively establishing rules of conduct, you will reduce the frequency with which you will have to deal with off-task behaviors. However, with 30 or more adolescents in a classroom, there may well be some incidents. The key to dealing effectively with disruptions or off-task behaviors in general is to maintain a clear, cool head by focusing on your purpose—to keep students engaged in worthwhile lessons. The following is an example of a teacher who was able to deal effectively with a rather serious disruption because she focused on her purpose and attacked the problem systematically:

Keith, a member of Ms. Umbach's ninth grade remedial math class, is working in a small group lesson with four other students playing multiplication bingo. When the game conductor calls out, "Seventeen times 33," the students begin computing and Dan exclaims, "Bingo!" Keith stands up and yells, "Dan, you stupid jerk! I was about to get bingo! You cheated!" With these words, Keith shoves Dan over and upsets everyone's game cards. Ms. Umbach has been completing paperwork at her desk when she hears Keith yell and then observes the incident. She arrives unhesitatingly on the scene, uses one hand to grab Keith by the arm, and briskly walks him out the classroom door into the hallway. "You wait here while I check to see if I can help Dan. He may be hurt," she says calmly to Keith, looking directly into his eyes. She immediately turns her back to the boy without giving him a chance to speak. She has already noted initially that Dan was not hurt, but she returns to the bingo scene where an audience has gathered around Dan who is beginning to express his intention of retaliating. Ms. Umbach interrupts Dan with, "I am sorry about what happened, but I am happy that you are not hurt." Before anyone can complain about Keith or before Dan can make any further threats, the teacher continues, "Tanya and Bart, I would appreciate your picking up this mess and setting up the bingo game again. We'll start over with four players." Then she raises her voice, saying, "Everyone return to your work. Thank you."

Ms. Umbach quickly returns to Keith in the hall and says, "I do not have time now to deal with the way you behaved during multiplication bingo. Right now, I have a class to teach and you have to continue practicing multiplication. We'll have time to discuss how we can stop these disruptions before the first bell tomorrow morning. As soon as your bus arrives tomorrow, I want you to meet me at my desk. Will you remember or should I call your house tonight to remind you?" Keith: "I'll remember." Ms. Umbach: "Good! Now, you still need to work on your multiplication. We have about 12 minutes to do that. Go get your workbook and bring it to me at my desk." Keith complies and Ms. Umbach directs him to complete a multiplication exercise at a table away from other students. The multiplication exercise is a drill on the same skills that the bingo game was designed to develop.

After school that day, Ms. Umbach has the following thoughts:

Well, I bought myself some time to decide what to do about Keith's outbursts and fighting! ... I took a chance grabbing him the way I did; with his temper he might have turned on me. And then what would have happened? ... Let's see, this is at least the third such display that's occurred while Keith was supposed to be doing small group work. I don't know if he's always been the cause, but he's always been in the middle ... That's not important. What is important is to prevent a recurrence before somebody gets hurt ... I'll just remove him from any small group work, as I did today. I hope he didn't think I was punishing him by assigning the workbook multiplication ... But he must learn that antisocial behavior will not be tolerated in my classroom ... Tomorrow, maybe I should explain my dilemma to him and ask what he would do to solve the problem if he were in my place. That tactic worked well when I tried it with Lynwood ... But no, Keith isn't ready for that yet; he's too defensive. Okay, here's what I'll try:

1. Tomorrow, I will not even try to explain my reasons for what I'm doing (that will only give Keith a chance to argue and act defensively and I don't need that). I will simply tell him what we're going to do and not try to defend the plan.

2. Whenever he would normally be doing small group work, I will assign him to work by himself at a table away from the others. His assignment will be comparable in content and, when possible, will have a goal similar to what he would be doing in the small group.

3. I'll observe for indicators that he will be more willing to cooperate in group activities.

4. As I see encouraging indications, I will gradually work him back in with the other students. But I will begin very slowly and only with brief, noncompetitive-type activities.

Now I'd better prepare for this ... What should I do if he doesn't show up before school tomorrow? ...

Ms. Umbach viewed the problem of eliminating the undesirable behavior just as she would view the question of helping a student to achieve a learning objective. By applying teaching techniques to the task of teaching students to choose engaged behaviors instead of off-task behaviors, she was able to focus her time, energy, and thought on the real issues at hand. She did not, for example, try to moralize to Keith about the evils of fighting. She was realistic enough to know that such lecturing would fall on deaf ears.

Teachers who do not systematically focus on the behavior to be altered—for example, Ms. Blythe in the first anecdote in Chapter 5 (page 38)—tend to compound difficulties by dwelling on irrelevant issues. Teachers who fail to focus on the goal of getting and keeping students engaged in lessons feel offended when students become disruptive or do not pay attention. When this happens, there is a tendency to retaliate, "to put students in their places." Teachers who keep their goal in mind are far more likely to realize that students are usually not threatening them by off-task behavior, nor are students off task in order to traumatize them.

By keeping their purpose in mind, teachers find it easier to remember that students get off task because they are bored, want to call attention to themselves, feel threatened, or feel frustrated or because of some other reason that is not a personal attack on the teacher.

16 SUGGESTIONS TO KEEP IN MIND

Here are 16 suggestions for you to consider when confronted with students who are off task.

1. Deal with off-task behavior as you would with any other student need.

Suppose that you are trying to teach your students about something other than how to read (e.g., principles of nutrition). However, your lesson plan depends on the students' comprehending what they read from a textbook assignment. One of your students appears to lack the reading skill to comprehend the necessary information from the reading assignment. Visualize yourself dealing with this all-too-familiar situation. Are you angry with this student for not knowing how to read as well as you would like?

My guess is that rather than reacting in anger to the lack of reading proficiency, you would take steps either to help the student improve the reading skills or to work around the difficulty (e.g., by finding a means to communicate the information that didn't depend on reading skill).

Now suppose that you are trying to teach your students something other than how to behave (e.g., principles of nutrition). However, your lesson plan depends on the students' cooperatively engaging in the learning activity you have designed for them. One of your students talks when it is time to listen and refuses to follow your directions for attempting an assignment. Visualize yourself dealing with this all-too-familiar situation. Are you angry with this student for not cooperating with you?

Most of us are more likely to react in anger to students' lack of cooperative, on-task behaviors than to their lack of some prerequisite academic skill. But being on task is also prerequisite to learning and needs to be taught to students just like a prerequisite academic skill. Students learn to supplant off-task behaviors with requisite on-task behaviors when we respond to their displays of off-task behaviors with sound, systematic pedagogical techniques, not when we respond out of anger. Research-based methods for teaching off-task students to be on task are reported in the professional literature (see, e.g., 14; 36; 38; 91, pp. 183–286; 92; 100; 107). For each incident of off-task behavior, these methods generally require you to:

a. *Determine whether the off-task behavior is disruptive to other students in the class.* For a nondisruptive off-task behavior (e.g., a student daydreaming), you may not feel compelled to respond as quickly as you would for a disruptive off-task behavior (e.g., a student talking loudly during a planned quiet reading period). Thus, for cases of nondisruptive off-task behaviors, you enjoy more flexibility as to *when* you intervene.

b. *Determine if the off-task behavior is part of a habitual pattern or only an isolated incident.* Your initial response to an incident of off-task behavior is to take action that will get the students back on task. Ms. Umbach in the anecdote on page 46 did this by walking Keith out of the room, checking on Dan, and then quickly getting the learning activity restarted. But for cases in which the off-task behavior is part of a continuing pattern, you also need to apply strategies to teach the student(s) to supplant the undesirable habit with a pattern of on-task behaviors. Ms. Umbach recognized that Keith's misbehavior was part of a pattern that she should develop strategies to break.

Off-task behavior *patterns* are, of course, more difficult to terminate than isolated incidents. However, you usually have the luxury of taking time to plan strategies for intervening in patterns, whereas isolated off-task behaviors typically need to be dealt with as they occur. Principles of behavior modification (see, e.g., 14; 91, pp.

215–31; 127) are applicable in the design of methods for (1) helping students break off-task behavior patterns and (2) preventing students' isolated displays of off-task behaviors from becoming habitual.

c. *Decide on objectives*. Just as you establish objectives for academic lessons, so should your strategy for responding to an off-task behavior systematically target one or more specific objectives. Ms. Umbach's initial objectives were to terminate the violent altercation, restore order, redirect attention away from Keith and any retaliatory thoughts Dan might be harboring, and get students back to work. Later she focused on getting Keith to control his temper and cooperate in group activities.

d. *Plan a course of action for achieving the objectives.*

e. *Implement the plan.*

f. *Assess how well the objectives are achieved.*

In the following two examples, teachers systematically deal with off-task behaviors; the first is an isolated incidence, while the second involves a pattern of off-task behavior:

Mr. Groves is speaking to his science class about weather patterns when he notices two students, Cynthia and Greg, engaged in their own personal conversation. Without missing a word in his lecture, he moves between the students and continues explaining weather patterns. The two stop talking and appear to pay attention as long as Mr. Groves is between them. Five minutes later, with Mr. Groves speaking from another area of the room, Cynthia and Greg are conversing again. This time Mr. Groves goes over to them as he continues to lecture, picks up Greg's papers from the top of his desk, and motions Greg to follow him to another part of the room where there is a vacant desk. Mr. Groves places Greg's papers on the desk top, and Greg takes a seat. At no time during the incident did Mr. Groves speak directly to either Cynthia or Greg, nor did he miss a word in his discourse on weather patterns.

Later in the day, Mr. Groves thinks about what happened: "It was unusual for Cynthia and Greg to be talking in class like that. I wonder what motivated today's episode. Well, it doesn't make any difference as long as it doesn't become habitual. My strategy worked well today, but I hope I didn't give anybody the impression that I'll tolerate off-task talking because I didn't come down harder on them. I'll just make sure

50

I act quickly the next time something like this happens. If these isolated incidences go unchecked, they could turn into patterns."

Riley and Dustin, two eighth graders, are almost constant companions. Ms. Delnegro, their teacher, thinks of their relationship as healthy and doesn't want to discourage their friendship. However, they have developed a habit of talking, passing notes, giggling, and looking at one another during class that has become disruptive to many of the learning activities. In the past, she has treated incidences of their off-task talking as isolated behaviors. But now she decides to somehow get them to modify what she recognizes as a disruptive behavior pattern. After some thought, Ms. Delnegro formulates three alternative plans (91, p. 268):

1. Ms. Delnegro will confront the two with the problem they have been creating. In a private conference, she will tell Riley and Dustin that whenever she recognizes that they are talking at an inappropriate time, she will point to the time-out room where they are to go until the learning activity that they have disturbed is over.

2. Ms. Delnegro will routinely schedule "free talk" sessions after quiet learning activities. Participation in the free talk sessions, in which students may socialize within certain guidelines, will be contingent on all students' having quietly engaged in the previous learning activity. Time wasted during the planned learning activity due to disruptive talking is to be made up from time scheduled for the free talk session.

3. Whenever Riley and Dustin's talking disrupts a learning activity, Ms. Delnegro will use the timer she wears on her wrist to keep account of the time wasted. Riley and Dustin are to make up for the lost minutes after school that day. Riley's and Dustin's parents would have to agree to this plan, so they can cooperate in having the students get home on days they miss their buses.

Ms. Delnegro hasn't yet decided which of the three plans she will try first. She sees advantages in each. The first, she thinks, will work because she believes that Riley and Dustin do not like to be excluded from class activities and will soon "talk themselves out" in the time-out room (i.e., application of the principle of satiation) (53, pp. 137–53; 91, pp. 229–30). She believes that with the second, peer pressure would motivate Riley and Dustin to control their talking. The third plan utilizes the power of negative reinforcement (53, pp. 108–202; 91, pp. 41–46) because the boys would control when Ms. Delnegro stopped her timer.

---

2. Deal decisively with an off-task behavior, or don't deal with it at all.

In the anecdote in Chapter 5 (pages 40–41), Ms. Larsen should have used an effective method to teach Thelma and Emily to obey hall rules, or she should have ignored their running altogether. It is a waste of time and energy to use half-hearted attempts that do more harm than good. Jones (45) has found that teachers handle discipline problems far more effectively when they speak face-to-face, directly to students, than when they speak "over-the-shoulder" in a "matter-of-fact" tone. Let your students know that being on task is serious business. Compare the following two examples:

Mr. Daugs is diagramming the structure of the human heart on the chalkboard and explaining its functions as disruptive conversations among his eleventh graders break out in various parts of the classroom. Continuing to write on the board, Mr. Daugs looks over his shoulder and says, "Okay, knock it off. There's too much noise in here. Now, as I was saying, when venous blood returns to the ...Didn't I say to be quiet! Okay, as venous blood..." The level of talk rises again, and Mr. Daugs continues to respond in this half-hearted fashion. At one point, he reminds them that if they don't listen, they won't do well on tomorrow's test.

Mr. Allred is diagramming the structure of the human heart on the chalkboard and explaining its functions as disruptive conversations among his eleventh graders break out in various parts of the classroom. He calmly, but deliberately returns the chalk to its tray, pivots around to face the class, moves closer to the students, and says while moving his eyes from one student to the next, "It is senseless for me to try to explain the functions of the heart to you when you can't concentrate on what I'm saying because of the talking in the room. Please open your textbooks to page 121. Begin reading in the middle where it says 'Oxygenating Blood,' and then continue through page 133." One student raises her hand, and the following exchange occurs:

Mr. Allred: Yes, Rosa, what would you like to say?

Rosa: Are we still going to be tested on this tomorrow?

Mr. Allred: Yes, we will stick to the schedule.

Wen: But that's not fair. You didn't finish explaining it to us!

Mr. Allred: I agree that it is unfortunate I was unable to finish my explanation. But let's not discuss it any more right now, so you'll have time to finish the reading.

---

3. Control the time and place for dealing with disruptions.

In the anecdote beginning on page 46, Ms. Umbach focused her immediate efforts on getting the class back on task after Keith's disruption. She waited until she had time to work out a plan to deal with Keith in a setting that she could readily control. If she had tried to teach Keith not to be disruptive at the time and place of the incident, she would have had to contend with the following disadvantages:

a. She would have had to supervise the rest of the class and thus could not have given Keith her full attention.

b. She would have had little time for deciding what to do.

c. Both Ms. Umbach and Keith would not have had time to cool off.

d. Keith would have had an audience of peers whose perceptions were more important to him than whatever Ms. Umbach was trying to do, so he probably would have been thinking more about what *they* were thinking than about what she was saying.

Some teachers feel obliged to demonstrate their authority by dealing with a student who has been disruptive in front of the class. Such tactics should be reconsidered. Usually, it is more efficient first to get everyone back on task and then to deal with preventing future occurrences at a time and place that you can effectively control. Don't worry that students will think that the disrupter "got off." Word will get back to them that you handled the situation decisively.

4. Always leave students a face-saving way to terminate an incident.

Teachers are asking for trouble whenever they do anything that leads students to feel embarrassed in front of their peers. Many times in my teaching career students have made insulting remarks to me. In anger, I have been tempted to return such rudeness with a retort. Given that the student is an adolescent and the teacher an adult, it is not surprising that the student is vulnerable to a witty put-down by a teacher reacting to a student's misbehavior. But playing such verbal games detracts from the dignity of a businesslike learning environment and fuels conflicts. Here is an account of one unfortunate incident I observed in a junior high classroom:

In the course of giving directions to his class, Mr. Canisius says, "...And what can I do if the work is not done on time?..." In a barely audible voice, Charlie says, "You can go get ------." "What did you say?!" shouts Mr. Canisius. Charlie just looks around the room, grins sheepishly, and puts his head down. He says nothing. "What did you say?" repeats Mr. Canisius. "Nothing," whispers Charlie. "I didn't hear you," Mr. Canisius says in a much calmer voice, feeling more confident now that Charlie seems to be backing down. Charlie responds, "I said, 'Nothing.' I didn't say anything." "That's what I thought. I didn't think you said anything because you never say anything worth hearing!" retorts Mr. Canisius in a superior-sounding voice. Some class members look at one another and grin; others watch Charlie, wondering what he is going to do next. Suddenly Charlie looks directly at Mr. Canisius and blurts out, "I said, 'Go get ------!' So why don't you, instead of messing with me!"

By trying to outwit a student, Mr. Canisius turned a self-terminating incident into a major situation that jeopardized Charlie's position at the school. Mr. Canisius heard Charlie's original rude remark. What was his motive in asking, "What did you say?" What options did such a question leave the student? Initially, Charlie tried to terminate the incident by not responding to the question. But Mr. Canisius forced the issue, and Charlie provided him with the expected lie by denying what he had said. Getting Charlie to back down gave Mr. Canisius false confidence. Because an insecure adult tried to prove his "superiority" over an adolescent, the conflict exploded.

Mr. Canisius should have left Charlie a dignified way out of the unpleasant situation either by ignoring his original rudeness or by politely directing Charlie to visit with him at a time when the teacher could respond without Charlie's peers in attendance.

5. Terminate disruptions without playing detective.

In the previous anecdote, Mr. Canisius knew that Charlie was the source of the rude comment. Many times, however, teachers are unable to detect the source of disruptions. The following is an example of such a situation:

Some students in Mr. Babin's history class frequently amuse themselves while the teacher is talking by covertly screeching "Whoopwhoop!" Mr. Babin is habitually interrupted by the rude noise either when he is trying to explain something to the group or when he is working with an individual student. Initially, Mr. Babin reacted to the annoyance with, "All right! Who's the bird in here?" Often he has tried unsuccessfully to catch the culprits. More and more students are displaying their boldness with the cry and their cleverness at concealing the source.

In his frustration, Mr. Babin turns to Ms. Travis, a colleague, for advice. Ms. Travis indicates to him that the students don't really intend to make his life miserable (which is what he is allowing to happen), but they are simply relieving their boredom by playing a game of cat and mouse with him. Ms. Travis suggests that Mr. Babin quit trying to catch the culprits and thus put an end to the game. She advises him to design a plan for terminating the discourtesy without worrying about identifying the guilty. Ms. Travis tells him:

Make up your mind not to care who is making the rude noises. Schedule a portion of class time to confront them with the fact that you feel hurt by their rudeness. Tell them that you cannot teach effectively when they're making disruptive noises. But also tell them that you are responsible for seeing that they learn history. Therefore, when you're talking to any one or to all of the students and you hear that noise, stop and tell them that because they won't allow you to talk to them, you simply aren't going to try. Discontinue the explanation you were giving at the time of the interruption and write a note on the chalkboard directing them to read for themselves the material from the book that you had planned to cover in class. In the note, remind them of the date on which they will be tested on the material. Don't answer questions or give explanations until the next meeting period when you'll once again give them the opportunity to treat you courteously. Remember not to delay or delete material from the scheduled test.

I think that they'll quickly tire of trying to learn without your help. Then they'll start to put pressure on each other to stop the rude noises. Start each period fresh so grudges won't build from day to day.

6. **Utilize the help of colleagues, parents, and supervisors; don't be fooled by the "myth of the good teacher."**

In the previous anecdote, Mr. Babin sought the counsel of a trusted colleague. But some teachers are afraid to seek help from other adults because they are deluded by what Canter and Canter (17, pp. 6–7) refer to as the "myth of the good teacher." According to the myth, teachers who are really "good" can handle all their own discipline problems without outside help. Teachers suffering under this myth feel guilty for bothering others with problems they think of themselves as too weak to handle. In reality, consulting with colleagues is more a sign of professional behavior than it is a sign of weakness (91, pp. 120–24, 198–99). Furthermore, your supervisors are legally and ethically responsible for supporting your instructional efforts (93, 116, 118), and parents typically have greater influence over their children's behaviors than you do (17).

7. **Maintain professional confidences.**

Clearly distinguish between (1) the professional practice of conferring with trusted colleague teachers, authorized supervisors, and students' *own* parents and (2) the unprofessional practice of gossiping about students or sharing "discipline problem" anecdotes with unauthorized persons. Compare the professionalism of the behaviors of the teachers in the following two examples:

Here is a portion of a conversation between Ms. Scott and the father of Synda Alberts, one of her students:

Ms. Scott: I need you to work with me in helping to teach Synda to respect the space of her classmates. She has a tendency to entertain herself in class by doing annoying things like jabbing her neighbors with a pencil or grabbing things from their desks. It seems to be her way of being friendly, but it's very disturbing to my lessons.

Mr. Alberts: She's so fidgety. I've told her a million times, "Settle down; be more like your friend Margaret." Margaret seems so serene. I bet she doesn't give you trouble in class. Does she?

Ms. Scott: I'd rather not talk about other students' behaviors. It's Synda's behavior we need to work on.

Here is a portion of a conversation between Ms. White and the mother of Angus Murphy, one of her students:

Ms. White: Thank you so much for coming to the parent-teacher conference. It's a real pleasure to speak to the parent of one of my top students.

Ms. Murphy: What a nice thing for you to say! Angus is doing okay?

Ms. White: Okay! If I could get some of my other students to be half as cooperative as Angus, my life would be a breeze. Why just today, Peter Marcusen just wouldn't settle down in class. I had to call his name six times before I finally . . .

Trust between a teacher and students is an important ingredient in establishing a classroom climate that is conducive to cooperation and on-task behaviors. Teachers who violate that trust by gossiping about students risk the professional/client relationship that facilitates the efficient handling of discipline problems (91, pp. 106–107).

8. Have alternative lesson plans available for times when students do not cooperate as planned.

When conducting a planned lesson, you should expect students to cooperate with you and choose to be engaged in the learning activities. Your confident expectation increases the chances that they will cooperate. However, by being prepared in the event that some students refuse to cooperate, you guard against operating under the stress of the lesson getting "out of control." A well-designed learning activity should not be aborted simply because it is not going as smoothly as you would like. However, as Ms. Umbach (page 46) and Mr. Allred (pages 52–53) demonstrated, there is quite an advantage to having alternate and less enjoyable activities ready for times when students' off-task behaviors render your original plan unworkable. These alternate activities should target the same learning objectives as the original activities.

9. Work as diligently to decrease the incidence of nondisruptive off-task behaviors as to decrease the incidence of disruptions.

Nondisruptive off-task behaviors (e.g., mind-wandering, failing to attempt assignments, being under the influence of drugs during lessons, sleeping in class, and even cheating on tests) are sometimes disregarded because they do not necessarily interfere with the activities of the class as a whole. However, you need to be concerned with all forms of student nonengagement for the following reasons:

a. When students are off task, they are failing to benefit from your planned lesson and are thus diminishing their chances of achieving the learning goal. Your responsibility for helping them achieve learning goals includes helping them supplant off-task behaviors with on-task behaviors.

b. Because off-task behaviors interfere with learning, even nondisruptive students who are off task tend to fall behind in a lesson. Once students miss one part of a lesson, they are likely not to understand a subsequent part, even though they return to engaged behavior. And those who are unable to follow a lesson may well become bored and disruptive.

In the following anecdotes, one example of nondisruptive off-task behavior is mishandled, and one is handled well:

Ms. Searcy is explaining to her ninth grade science class how Darwin and Wallace each arrived at his theory of natural selection. Most of the class listens intently. Amy sits up straight, staring directly at Ms. Searcy as she imagines herself high on a horse galloping along a river bank. Ms. Searcy, who watches her students' faces as she lectures, notices the blank look in Amy's eyes. Suspicious that Amy is not "with her," she pauses and asks, "What do you think about that, Amy?" Amy: "...About what?" Ms. Searcy: "About what I said." Amy: "I don't know what you said." Ms. Searcy: "You don't know what I said! Were you daydreaming?" Amy: "I guess so." Ms. Searcy: "Amy, the daydreamer, off in a world of her own!... Okay! Let's listen from now on." Amy: "Yes, ma'am, I will."

"Off in a world of her own!... Amy, the daydreamer!" Amy thinks, still staring directly at Ms. Searcy and now nodding her head as if in agreement. She keeps pondering those words; she likes the sound of "a daydreamer... off in a world of her own."

Ms. Smith is explaining to her ninth grade science class how Darwin and Wallace each arrived at his theory of natural selection. Most of the class listens intently. Anita sits up straight, staring directly at Ms. Smith as she imagines herself high on a horse galloping along a river bank. Ms. Smith, who watches her students' faces as she lectures, notices the blank look in Anita's eyes. Suspicious that Anita is not "with her," she pauses and asks the class, "Why do you suppose Darwin waited so long before publishing his theory?... Anita?" Anita: "...What was the question?" Ms. Smith: "Please repeat the question for those of us who missed it, Michael." Michael: "You asked why Darwin took so long before publishing his stuff." Ms. Smith: "Thanks, Mike. What's your opinion, Debbie?" Debbie gives her opinion, and the lecture/discussion continues. Ms. Smith subtly observes Anita to see if her strategy worked.

---

10. Allow students to recognize for themselves the natural consequences of not attempting assignments or failing to participate in lessons.

It is not unusual for some teachers to punish students or to artificially manipulate their grades because the students fail to attempt assignments or to participate in class activities. However, assignments that are really meaningful to students make such punishment or grade manipulation unnecessary.

In the following anecdote, Ms. Goldberg comes to realize that as long as her assignment benefited her students, it made no sense either to give "points toward their grades" for attempting assignments or to punish them for not doing assignments:

Ms. Goldberg, a mathematics teacher, uses a procedure in which each student's grade is determined by the number of points accumulated during a semester. Her students have two means of accumulating points: (1) half of the total possible points are based on their test scores; (2) the other half are awarded for homework that, when turned in on time, is scored according to the number of correct responses.

Ms. Goldberg discovers that a number of students receive high marks on their homework, but low marks on their test papers. Under her system, such students are able to pass the course. After analyzing the matter, she realizes that these students are either copying their homework from others or having others do it for them. Thus, she decides to change her grading procedures. She will annotate students' homework to provide them with feedback, but she will not grade their homework so that it influences their semester reports. Ms. Goldberg begins to make a concerted effort to assign homework and design tests so that completing homework will clearly be an effective way to prepare for tests.

To begin conditioning her students to the new system, she assigns homework one day and then administers a test the next that covers virtually the same material that they practiced for homework.

---

11. Never use corporal punishment.

There are times when teachers should physically restrain students to prevent them from injuring themselves, other students, or the teacher. But for teachers to intentionally inflict physical pain on a student for the purpose of making the student sorry for some misconduct is more harmful than helpful (22). Teachers who are familiar with relevant research findings and who value the welfare and well-being of their students will not resort to corporal punishment (84).

Although (1) many prominent professional organizations (e.g., the National Education Association, American Federation of Teachers, Council for Exceptional Children, and American Psychological Association) have issued statements adamantly opposing it in schools and (2) its use has been banned in schools in some countries and states (e.g., New South Wales in Australia and New Jersey in the United States), corporal punishment continues to be widely, but inconsistently, used in schools (110, 111, 124, 129).

Arguments for and against corporal punishment are presented in *Classroom Management Strategies: Gaining and Maintaining Students' Cooperation*:

Supporters of corporal punishment as a response to off-task school behavior in at least some circumstances provide the following arguments:

1. There is the saying, "Spare the rod and spoil the child."

2. The *Bible* (e.g., Prov. 13:24, 12:15, 23:13) supports corporal punishment as a means of moral development.

3. What else works?

4. Some students do not understand anything else.

5. Teachers need to be able to protect themselves.

6. Corporal punishment builds character and, for boys, masculinity.

7. There are harsher, more dangerous forms of punishment, such as sustained psychological embarrassment.

8. Students want corporal punishment. It provides the firm guidance that students need to feel secure.

9. It leads students to respect teachers and to have respect for authority.

10. Parents want their children disciplined at school.

11. Unlike many other ways of handling off-task behaviors, corporal punishment can be immediately administered so that the student can quickly return to the business of being engaged in learning activities.

12. Using corporal punishment for one student's off-task behavior may deter others from modeling that off-task behavior.

13. Federal courts have consistently upheld the right of school officials to utilize corporal punishment.

14. The abuses of corporal punishment can be prevented by allowing its application only under clearly specified, strictly controlled circumstances. Different school districts have developed their own guidelines. The following is a sample of rules from the guidelines of a variety of districts:

    a. Corporal punishment shall only be used as a last resort, after other more desirable means have failed.

    b. Corporal punishment may be administered only to students whose parents have provided the school with written permission.

    c. Corporal punishment may only be administered by the school principal or his or her designee.

    d. Corporal punishment shall be prescribed only for those who will profit from it.

    e. No student is required to submit to corporal punishment providing that he or she is willing to accept the alternative noncorporal punishment that is prescribed by the school discipline official.

    f. To give those involved a "cooling off" period, no corporal punishment may be administered within one hour from when the violation that is to be punished occurred.

    g. Whenever corporal punishment is administered at least two professional adults must be present.

    h. Corporal punishment may be administered only for certain student offenses as specified in the "Disciplinary Code Handbook."

    i. Corporal punishment may be administered to boys only.

    j. The severity of corporal punishment is strictly limited.

The arguments provided by those opposed to any form of corporal punishment in schools seem more compelling:

1. Opposition to corporal punishment is *not* opposition to firm, strict discipline. "Sparing the rod" does not mean "spoiling the child" if other, more effective means for handling misbehaviors are employed.

2. Research does not support the notion that corporal punishment is an effective tool in teaching students to supplant off-task behaviors with on-task behaviors (89).

3. Corporal punishment is an extremely destructive form of contrived punishment. Even when it serves to discourage one misbehavior, the more long ranged side effects can be far less desirable than the original misbehavior (43). Welsh (126) reports that no one has ever demonstrated the utility of spanking a child and, "When spanking does work, it is not unlike whacking your watch with your hand to make it tick. This crude procedure may work for a while, but the long-term consequence of hitting one's watch is likely to be detrimental to the delicate mechanism. Our research suggests that the watch analogy also holds for whacking children." The association between children experiencing corporal punishment and their development of aggressive or violent behavior patterns is both well-documented and well-publicized (86, 87, 88, 98, 123, 126).

4. Corporal punishment shatters any semblance of a businesslike classroom climate in which mutual respect, cooperation, and seriousness of purpose prevail (51, 119, 120). The sanctity of the learning environment is violated whenever any sort of violent behavior is tolerated. Corporal punishment is not only tolerated violence; it is condoned violence that is modeled by school personnel.

5. Research findings indicate that school personnel who rely on corporal punishment tend to be less experienced, more close-minded, more neurotic, less thoughtful, and more impulsive than their counterparts who do not use corporal punishment (113).

Assuming that it is legal to use corporal punishment in your school, under what circumstances should you either administer it yourself or refer students to another who is authorized to administer it? Although it is still commonly used and may sometimes seem to be a swift, decisive way of dealing with certain off-task behaviors, there are no circumstances when you should depend on corporal punishment. How can one possibly resolve the inconsistency between using corporal punishment and being a professional educator once the following have been considered: (1) the availability of more effective alternatives to dealing with off-task behaviors, (2) the long-range side effects of corporal punishment, and (3) its corrupting influence on the businesslike air of respect and cooperation that contributes so much to maintaining students on-task and engaged in learning activities? (91, pp. 206–208)*

12. Don't try to build a student's character when you should be trying only to keep him/her engaged in a lesson.

In the first anecdote in this chapter, Ms. Umbach did not try to teach Keith about the evils of fighting; she concentrated on teaching him not to fight in her classroom. She recognized her responsibility for keeping students engaged in lessons that lead them to achieve stated learning objectives. She believes that developing students' characters and turning them into moral, upstanding citizens fall outside the realm of both her responsibilities and her capabilities as a teacher. Her method of stopping the clash between Keith and Dan and efficiently getting everyone reengaged in the learning activity was successful, at least in part, because she focused on her teaching objectives and didn't get sidetracked trying to build Keith's character.

The teacher in the following example approaches another serious problem with a similar attitude:

Libba, an eleventh grader, stops at a convenience store on her way to school. She buys three cans of beer and consumes them before her 8:45 a.m. homeroom period. Neither her homeroom teacher nor her first period history teacher notices anything strange in her behavior. However, as second period begins, she appears tipsy to Mr. Wagoner, her science teacher. Mr. Wagoner directs two students to begin setting up an experiment that he plans to demonstrate to the class. While they are doing this, he subtly beckons Libba to the doorway and out in the hall. Detecting the odor of alcohol on her breath, he says, "It's your business if you want to mess up your own life. But it's my business to teach you science, and I can't teach it to you when you're in that condition. When we've completed this conversation, you go back to your desk. Just keep quiet and concentrate on facing straight ahead... Did you hear me?" Libba: "Yes, sir." Mr. Wagoner: "Fine. Tomorrow

*From *Classroom Management Strategies: Gaining and Maintaining Students' Cooperation* by James S. Cangelosi. Copyright © 1988 by Longman Publishing. Reprinted with permission.

morning, come to this room at 8:15. We'll discuss the matter then. Can you remember to be here, or should I remind you with a call tonight?" Libba: "I'll remember; I'll be here."

At 8:15 the next morning, Libba makes her appointment, and Mr. Wagoner tells her, "If you ever come into my class again while under the influence of alcohol or any other drug, I will immediately send you to Ms. Swindle's office. I will inform Mr. Giradeau that I refuse to teach you in that condition. And I will inform your parents of the situation. Do you understand?" Libba: "Yes, but I'm not the only..." Mr. Wagoner (interrupting): "I am not talking with you about others, only you. I don't discuss your problems with other students, and I won't discuss theirs with you. Do you understand?" Libba: "Yes!" Mr. Wagoner: "Yesterday while you were 'out of it,' we were analyzing this experiment that is described here in my teacher's manual. I want you to take my manual home tonight and analyze the experiment as it is described on pages 79 through 84. Bring in your results, and I'll be happy to give you feedback on them as soon as I find the time. That should catch you up with the rest of the class. You won't be behind anymore. Okay?" Libba: "Okay." Mr. Wagoner: "See you in class. Keep smiling."

---

13. Deal with student drug and alcohol abuse from the perspective of its impact on student engagement in lessons.

Boredom, lack of confidence, frustration, fatigue, lack of motivation, hyperactive personalities, and nonacademic interests are just some of the many factors influencing students to be off task, even during well-designed, expertly conducted lessons. Attending school either high on drugs or depressed from drugs is just one more factor to add to the list of influences that make it difficult for students to be on task and engaged in learning activities. That factor is given special attention herein, not because it is any more pervasive than the others, but because (a) its influence seems to be increasing at an alarming rate (101, 122) and (b) information on how to deal with students who abuse drugs has only recently become available (see, e.g., 91, pp. 245-55; 112; 121).

Teachers respond to their students' misuse of drugs in a variety of ways (91, pp. 245-51):

a. Some teachers are unaware of their students' drug use although it is occurring at their schools and interfering with the success of their lessons. Such teachers remain naive because they view their classes as faceless masses rather than as individual unique personalities. Both subtle and dramatic personality swings of individual students

64

go undetected. These teachers tend to think of themselves as teaching academic content (e.g., European literature or trigonometry) rather than students, some of whom may be bright-eyed while others are in a glassy-eyed stupor.

b. There are teachers who simply lack knowledge about drug abuse and about the prospect of drug abusers in their classroom. The best-intentioned of these teachers are willing to attend drug awareness seminars and study some of the recently published materials on drug abuse among adolescent and preadolescent students. Other teachers from this group are so frightened by the thought of being around "junkies" and "dope addicts" that they take a "what I don't know won't hurt me" attitude.

c. It may be difficult to believe, but some teachers actually welcome the mellow, nondisruptive behaviors displayed by many students when under the influence of certain types of drugs (e.g., marijuana and barbiturates). One teacher I interviewed represented the thinking of most of those in this group when she said, "I wish he didn't use drugs at all, but I'd rather have him doped up than misbehaving. . . . He can sleep it off in my class. That way, he's not disturbing those who want to learn. I can't control their habits, so why try?"

d. There are teachers who conduct personal crusades against the evils of drugs. They moralize to students about drug abuse, but their preachy tactics are usually ineffectual, serving only to make themselves feel better that they are at least trying to do something about the problem.

e. There are an increasing number of teachers who, instead of moralizing about the evils of drugs, help to stem drug abuse among their students by doing three things:

1) They alter curricula so that specific units about drugs are taught and so that problems involving drugs are used to intrinsically motivate students to engage in lessons in subjects such as science, social studies, health and physical education, mathematics, language arts, and music. In other words they use *problem-solving lessons* (see Chapter 3 of this book) to teach their students to apply the power of an academic subject (e.g., mathematics) to make informed, prudent choices about drug use.

2) They arrange for students to have access to research-based information about drug use. The information may be provided by

bringing specialists into the school as guest speakers, supplying the library with up-to-date literature, or having a school "drug information" week.

3) They attempt to counsel students who appear to be abusing drugs to seek help (e.g., through a drug treatment program).

f. Many teachers realize they cannot be "all things" to their students, so they concentrate on helping them attain only those goals for which they are responsible. But they also understand that drug abuse interferes with their students' engagement in lessons. Therefore, they don't try to control students' drug abuse outside of their classrooms; rather, they only try to teach them to choose not to be under the influence of such substances when under their supervision. This was the stance Mr. Wagoner took with Libba in the previous anecdote.

You are advised to (a) become as knowledgeable as possible about student drug abuse by participating in drug awareness seminars and by reading some of the recently published literature on the subject (see, e.g., 91, 112, 121, 122) and (b) approach the problem as do either of the last two groups of teachers in the above list.

14. Never lose sight of the fact that each person controls her or his own actions.

Factors such as drug abuse, boredom, poor parenting, hyperactive personalities, and lack of confidence help explain why students misbehave in schools. Understanding these factors helps us to systematically devise methods to teach students to cooperate, behave, and be on task. However, our awareness of contributing factors should not be confused with excusing or tolerating misbehaviors. Consider the following exchange between two teachers:

Mr. Hearns: It's only the first week of school, and I've already run into a serious discipline problem! Can you help me work out a solution?

Ms. Ayers: Tell me about it.

Mr. Hearns: Do you know Gaynell Hayes?

Ms. Ayers: I'll never forget him after what I went through with him last year.

Mr. Hearns: Well, he's yet to turn in an assignment, and when I

66

asked him about it today, he told me it was up a certain part of his anatomy and I was welcome to go up and get it.

Ms. Ayers: What happened next?

Mr. Hearns: A few of the kids started laughing, but most of them seemed real uncomfortable. I told him I won't tolerate that kind of talk and directed him to wait for me in the office. He said, "Fine," and left, but he never showed up in the office. Apparently, he just skipped out.

Ms. Ayers: And what are you thinking of doing next?

Mr. Hearns: He's going to have to work out some sort of contingency plan to earn his way back into my class. But I don't want him showing up tomorrow until we've worked it out. I thought I'd call him tonight to set up a meeting before he comes back into class.

Ms. Ayers: I doubt if you'll be able to reach him by phone. He works pretty late hours.

Mr. Hearns: What's a kid like that doing with a late-night job?

Ms. Ayers: Well, Gaynell has got some real problems. He's moved back and forth between his parents' home and foster homes. He has a history of being abused. He's trying to earn enough money to support himself just to get out from under his so-called "parents"! It's really a sad situation.

Mr. Hearns: Gee! I'm glad you told me. That explains why he doesn't do his homework. No wonder he was hostile with me. He does well just to make it to school. I shouldn't have gotten angry with him. I'm not going to expect so much of him.

Ms. Ayers: Now, wait a minute! We would be shortchanging him terribly by expecting less of him than of other students. We may be his only hope for learning civil conduct and whatever else we're supposed to teach these kids. Don't you dare let him get away with missing assignments and rude behavior!

Mr. Hearns: But with his circumstances, he can't help but . . .

Ms. Ayers: Of course he can control his own behavior. He may be operating under unfavorable circumstances, and it's good for us to understand that, but he can still manage his own behavior.

Mr. Hearns: So if I can't get hold of him tonight, I'll intercept him in the morning and . . .

As I stated elsewhere:

Canter (95), Dreikurs (27), Ginott (35), Glasser (36), Gordon (38), and most other purveyors of thought on classroom discipline emphasize that each and every individual is responsible and held accountable for her or his own behaviors. Except for the relatively unusual cases where one person physically accosts another, one person cannot *make* another do something. Once students realize this, they are disarmed of virtually all of their excuses for misconduct. In order to lead students to understand that only they are in control of their own conduct, you should consistently use language that is free of suggestions that one person can control another. In other words, purge your language of statements such as these: "Be careful of what you say or you'll make Mia feel bad." "He made me lose control." "You made Allen cry." "Fred, don't get Tommy into trouble." "She got me so mad." "Vernon just can't get along without Martha." "She makes me happy."

Such language should be replaced with: "Be careful of what you say or Mia may think you don't enjoy her company." "I didn't maintain control when I saw what he did." "Allen was so unhappy with what you said that he cried." "Fred, don't encourage Tommy to do something he shouldn't." "I got so mad when I thought of what she did." "Vernon depends on Martha for help." "I'm happy to be with her."

Remind students that they control their own behaviors when they say such things as: "I did it because everybody wanted me to." "She hurts my feelings." "Make me happy." (91, pp. 98–99)*

15. Maintain your options; avoid "playing your last card."

Understand the extent and limits of your authority as a teacher. Never threaten a student with something if you cannot follow through. For example, if you tell a student, "Either sit down and start your work, or I'll make sure you never see the inside of this classroom again!" what are you going to do if the student refuses? You have extended your authority as far as it can reach. You have exhausted your options. Obtain the help of supervisors *before* you run out of ways to deal with undesirable situations.

16. Know yourself and know your students.

Continually examine your own motives for dealing with students. Be receptive to individual differences. Measures that are effective with one may be disastrous with another. Be conservative in trying out new ideas with an entire group until you know the students and have found the

---

*From *Classroom Management Strategies: Gaining and Maintaining Students' Cooperation* by James S. Cangelosi. Copyright © 1988 by Longman Publishing. Reprinted with permission.

ideas to be workable with the individuals you know best. On the other hand, don't give up on an idea because it won't work for all students all the time.

The last of these 16 suggestions is perhaps the most important of all. The better you understand yourself and your students, the better you will be able to elicit your students' cooperation and respond sensitively, flexibly, decisively, and effectively to discipline problems whenever they do occur.

BIBLIOGRAPHY

1. Alschuler, A. S., et al., eds. *Teacher Burnout*. Washington, D.C.: National Education Association, 1980.

2. Anderson, L.; Evertson, C.; and Emmer, E. "Dimensions in Classroom Management Derived from Recent Research." *Journal of Curriculum Studies* 12 (1980): 343–56.

3. Arlin, M. "Teacher Transitions Can Disrupt Time Flow in Classrooms." *American Educational Research Journal* 16 (1979): 42–56.

4. Arnold, D.; Atwood, R.; and Rogers, V. "Questions and Response Levels and Lapse Time Intervals." *Journal of Experimental Education* 43 (1974): 11–15.

5. Berlinger, D. "Changing Academic Learning Time: Clinical Intervention in Four Classrooms." Paper presented at annual meeting of American Educational Research Association, 1978.

6. Blackham, G. J., and Silberman, A. *Modification of Child and Adolescent Behavior*. Belmont, Calif.: Wadsworth Publishing Co., 1980.

7. Bloom, B. S. *Human Characteristics and School Learning*. New York: McGraw-Hill Book Co., 1976.

8. Bloom, R. B. "Teachers and Students in Conflict: The CREED Approach." *Phi Delta Kappan* 61 (1980): 624–26.

9. Borg, W. R. "Time and School Learning." In *Time to Learn*, edited by Carolyn Denham and Ann Lieberman. Washington, D.C.: National Institute of Education and California Commission on Teacher Preparation and Licensing, 1980.

10. Brophy, J., and Evertson, C. *Learning from Teaching: A Developmental Perspective*. Boston: Allyn and Bacon, 1976.

11. _____, and Putnam, J. "Classroom Management in the Elementary Grades." In *Classroom Management*, edited by D. Duke. Chicago: University of Chicago Press, 1979.

12. _____, and Rohrkemper, M. *Teachers' Specific Strategies for Dealing with Hostile and Aggressive Students*. Research Series Number 86. East Lansing, Mich.: Institute for Research on Teaching, Michigan State University, 1980.

13. _____, and _____. "The Influence of Problem-Ownership on Teacher Perceptions of and Strategies for Coping with Problem Students." *Journal of Educational Psychology* 73 (1981): 295–311.

14. Brown, D. *Changing Student Behavior: A New Approach to Discipline.* Dubuque, Iowa: William C. Brown Co., 1971.

15. Cangelosi, J. S. *Project G.R.E.A.T. Needs Assessment Report.* Tallahassee: Florida Department of Education, 1980.

16. ———. *Management and Evaluation: An Inductive Approach for Teachers.* Dubuque, Iowa: William C. Brown Co., 1982.

17. Canter, L., and Canter, M. *Assertive Discipline.* Los Angeles: Canter and Associates, 1976.

18. Carnine, D. W. "Effects of Two Teacher-Preparation Rates on Off-Task Behavior, Answering Correctly and Participation." *Journal of Applied Behavior Analysis* 9 (1974): 199–206.

19. Charles, C. M. *Building Classroom Discipline.* New York: Longman, 1981.

20. Crawford, J., and Robinson, C. *The Empirically Defined Domain of Effective Classroom Management: Final Report.* Princeton, N.J.: Educational Testing Service, 1981.

21. Crocker, R., et al. "An Experimental Study of Teacher Control in Sixth Grade Science Classes." Paper presented at annual meeting of National Association for Research in Science Teaching, 1977.

22. Curwin, R., and Mendler, A. *The Discipline Book: A Complete Guide to School and Classroom Management.* Reston, Va.: Reston Publishing Co., 1980.

23. Denham, C., and Lieberman, A., eds. *Time to Learn.* Washington, D.C.: National Institute of Education and California Commission on Teacher Preparation and Licensing, 1980.

23a. Dishon, Dee, and O'Leary, Pat Wilson. *Guidebook for Cooperative Learning: A Technique for Creating More Effective Schools.* Holmes Beach, Fla.: Learning Publications, 1984.

24. Dobson, J. *Dare to Discipline.* Wheaton, Ill.: Tyndale House Publishers, 1970.

25. Doyle, W. *Classroom Management.* West Lafayette, Ind.: Kappa Delta Pi, 1980.

26. Dreikurs, R., and Cassel, P. *Discipline Without Tears.* New York: Hawthorne Books, 1972.

27. ———; Grunwald, B.; and Pepper, F. *Maintaining Sanity in the Classroom.* New York: Harper and Row, 1981.

28. Emmer, E., and Evertson, C. "Synthesis of Research on Classroom Management." *Educational Leadership* (1981): 342–47.

29. Epstein, C. *Classroom Management and Teaching: Persistent Problems and Rational Solutions.* Reston, Va.: Reston Publishing Co., 1979.

30. Ernst, K. *Games Students Play.* Millbrae, Calif.: Celestial Arts Pubishing, 1979.

31. Fisher, C., et al. "Teaching Behaviors, Academic Learning Time and Student Achievement: Final Report of Phase III-B, Beginning Teacher Evaluation Study." Technical Report V-1. In *Beginning Teacher Evaluation Study.* San Francisco: Far West Regional Laboratory of Educational Research and Development, 1978.

32. Fraisee, P. *The Psychology of Time.* Westport, Conn.: Greenwood Press, 1975.

33. Galloway, D. *Case Studies in Classroom Management.* London: Longman Group Ltd., 1976.

34. Gil, D. G. "Child Abuse: Levels of Manifestation, Causal Dimensions, and Primary Prevention." *Victimology* 2 (Summer 1977): 186–94.

35. Ginott, H. G. *Teacher and Child: A Book for Parents and Teachers.* New York: Macmillan Co., 1972.

36. Glasser, W. *Schools Without Failure.* New York: Harper and Row, 1969.

37. Goldstein, J., and Weber, W. "Teacher Managerial Behaviors and Student On-Task Behavior." Paper presented at annual meeting of American Educational Research Association, 1979.

38. Gordon, T., with Burch, N. *T.E.T.: Teacher Effectiveness Training.* New York: Peter H. Wyden Publisher, 1974.

39. Grey, L. *Discipline Without Fear.* New York: Hawthorne Books, 1974.

40. Gudmundsen, W.; Williams, W.; and Lybbert, R. *You Can Control Your Class.* Salt Lake City, Utah: Class Control Associates, 1978.

41. Harris, T. A. *I'm Okay, You're Okay.* New York: Harper and Row, 1969.

42. Hoover, K. H. "Motivation-Discipline Techniques." *Secondary/Middle School Teaching: A Handbook for Beginning Teachers and Teacher Self-Renewal.* Boston: Allyn and Bacon, 1977.

43. Hyman, I., and Wise, J., eds. *Corporal Punishment in American Education: Readings in History, Practice, and Alternatives.* Philadelphia: Temple University Press, 1979.

44. Jacobsen, D., et al. *Methods for Teaching: A Skills Approach.* Columbus, Ohio: Charles E. Merrill Publishing Co., 1981.

45. Jones, F. H. "The Gentle Art of Classroom Discipline." *Principal* 58 (June 1979): 26–32.

46. Jones. V. F. *Adolescents with Behavior Problems: Strategies for Teaching, Counseling, and Parent Involvement.* Boston: Allyn and Bacon, 1980.

47. Joyce, B., and Weil, M. *Models of Teaching.* 2d ed. Englewood Cliffs, N.J.: Prentice-Hall, 1980.

48. Karweit, N., and Slavin, R. "Time-On-Task: Issues of Timing, Sampling, and Definition." *Journal of Educational Psychology* 74 (1982): 844–51.

49. Kerr, M., and Nelson, C. M. *Strategies for Managing Behavior Problems in the Classroom.* Columbus, Ohio: Charles E. Merrill Publishing Co., 1983.

50. Kohlberg, L., and Turiel, E. *Research in Moral Development: A Cognitive Developmental Approach.* New York: Holt, Rinehart, and Winston, 1971.

51. Kohut, S., Jr., and Range, D. G. *Classroom Discipline: Case Studies and Viewpoints.* Washington, D.C.: National Education Association, 1979.

52. Krajewski, R. J., and Shuman, R. B. *The Beginning Teacher: A Practical Guide to Problem Solving.* Washington, D.C.: National Education Association, 1979.

53. Krumboltz, J., and Krumboltz, H. *Changing Children's Behavior.* Englewood Cliffs, N.J.: Prentice-Hall, 1972.

54. Loo, C. M. "The Differential Effects of Spatial Density on Low and High Scorers on Behavior Problem Indices." Paper presented at annual meeting of Western Psychological Association, Seattle, Wash., 1979.

55. Madsen, C. H., Jr., and Madsen, C. K. *Teaching Discipline: A Positive Approach for Educational Development.* Boston: Allyn and Bacon, 1981.

56. McDaniel, T. R. "Exploring Alternatives to Punishment: The Keys to Effective Discipline." *Phi Delta Kappan* 61 (1980): 455–58.

56a. Moorman, Chick, and Dishon, Dee. *Our Classroom: We Can Learn Together.* Englewood Cliffs, N.J.: Prentice-Hall, 1983.

57. National Education Association. *Discipline and Learning: An Inquiry into Student-Teacher Relationships.* Washington, D.C.: National Education Association, 1977.

58. O'Banion, D., and Whaley, D. *Behavior Contracting: Arranging Contingencies of Reinforcement.* New York: Springer Publishing Co., 1981.

59. O'Leary, K., and O'Leary, S., eds. *Classroom Management: The Successful Use of Behavior Modification.* Elmsford, N.Y.: Pergamon Press, 1977.

60. Osborn, D. K., and Osborn, J. D. *Discipline and Classroom Management.* Athens, Ga.: Education Associates, 1981.

61. Presbie, R. J., and Brown, P. L. *Behavior Modification*. Washington, D.C.: National Education Association, 1980.

62. Reynolds, R. E., and Anderson, R. C. "Influences of Questions on the Allocation of Attention During Reading." *Journal of Educational Psychology* 74 (1982): 623–32.

63. Rivers, L. W. *The Disruptive Student and the Teacher*. Washington, D.C.: National Education Association, 1983.

64. Robert, S. C., ed. *Robert's Rules of Order*. Glenview, Ill.: Scott, Foresman, 1970.

65. Rogers, C. R. *Freedom to Learn*. Columbus, Ohio: Charles E. Merrill Publishing Co., 1969.

66. Rohrkemper, M., and Brophy, J. *Teachers' General Strategies for Dealing with Problem Students*. Research Series Number 87. East Lansing, Mich.: Institute for Research on Teaching, Michigan State University, 1980.

67. Saunders, M. *Class Control and Behavior Problems*. Maidenhead, Berkshire, England: McGraw-Hill Book Co. (UK), Ltd., 1979.

68. Schmuck, R.; Chesler, M.; and Lippit, R. *Problem Solving to Improve Classroom Learning*. Chicago: Science Research Associates, 1966.

69. Slavin, R. E. *Cooperative Learning: Student Teams*. Washington, D.C.: National Education Association, 1982.

70. _____. *Student Team Learning: An Overview and Practical Guide*. Washington, D.C.: National Education Association, 1983.

71. Swick, K. J. *Disruptive Student Behavior in the Classroom*. Washington, D.C.: National Education Association, 1980.

72. _____. *Maintaining Productive Student Behavior*. Rev. ed. Washington, D.C.: National Education Association, 1981.

73. _____, and Hanley, P. E. *Stress and the Classroom Teacher*. Washington, D.C.: National Education Association, 1980.

74. _____, and _____. *Teacher Renewal: Revitalization of Classroom Teachers*. Washington, D.C.: National Education Association, 1983.

75. Van Horn, K. "The Effects of the Utah Pupil/Teacher Self-Concept Program on the Invitational Verbal Behavior of Secondary Teachers." Paper presented at 1983 Alliance for Invitational Education, Greensboro, N.C.

76. Weber, W., with Roff, L. *The Classroom Management Project: A Technical Report*. Princeton, N.J.: Educational Testing Service, 1982.

77. Weber, W., et al. *Classroom Management: Reviews of the Teacher Education and Research Literature*. Princeton, N.J.: Educational Testing Service, 1983.

78. Weiner, E. H., ed. *Discipline in the Classroom*. 2d rev. ed. Washington, D.C.: National Education Association, 1980.

79. Wilen, W. W. *Questioning Skills, for Teachers*. Washington, D.C.: National Education Association, 1982.

80. Wilhelms, F. T., and Gibson, D. W. "Grouping Research Offers Leads." *Educational Leadership* 18 (April 1961): 410–13+.

81. Williams, J. L. *Discipline in the Classroom*. Leaflet. Washington, D.C.: National Education Association, 1983.

82. Wlodkowski, R. J. *Motivation*. Rev. ed. Washington, D.C.: National Education Association, 1982.

83. _____. *Motivation and Teaching: A Practical Guide*. Washington, D.C.: National Education Association, 1984.

84. Wolfgang, C. H., and Glickman, C. D. *Solving Discipline Problems: Strategies for Classroom Teachers*. Boston: Allyn and Bacon, 1980.

ADDITIONAL REFERENCES
FOR THE SECOND EDITION

85. Abernathy, S.; Manera, E.; and Wright, R. "What Stresses Student Teachers Most?" *Clearing House* 58 (1985): 361–62.

86. Arzin, N. H.; Hake, D. G.; and Hutchinson, R. R. "Elicitation of Aggression by a Physical Blow." *Journal of Experimental Analysis of Behavior* 8 (1965): 55–57.

87. Arzin, N. H.; Hutchinson, R. R.; and Sallery, R. D. "Pain-Aggression toward Inanimate Objects." *Journal of Experimental Analysis of Behavior* 7 (1964): 223–28.

88. Bandura, A. "Behavior Modification through Modeling Procedures." In *Research in Behavior Modification*, edited by L. Krasner and L. P. Ullman, 310–40. New York: Holt, Rinehart & Winston, 1965.

89. Bongiovanni, A. F. "An Analysis of Research on Punishment and Its Relation to the Use of Corporal Punishment in the Schools." In *Corporal Punishment in American Education*, edited by I. A. Hyman and J. H. Wise, 351–72. Philadelphia: Temple University Press, 1979.

90. Bridges, E. M. *The Incompetent Teacher.* Philadelphia: Falmer Press, 1986.

91. Cangelosi, J. S. *Classroom Management Strategies: Gaining and Maintaining Students' Cooperation.* New York: Longman, 1988.

92. _____. "Behavior Management for Reading Lessons." In *Reading Instruction and the Effective Teacher*, edited by B. L. Hayes. Boston: Allyn and Bacon, in press.

93. _____. *Evaluating Classroom Instruction.* New York: Longman, in press.

94. Cangelosi, J. S.; Struyk, L. R.; Grimes, M. L.; and Duke, C. R. "Classroom Management Needs of Beginning Teachers." Paper presented at annual meeting of American Educational Research Association, New Orleans, 1988.

95. Canter, L. "Be an Assertive Teacher." *Instructor* 88 (1978): 60.

96. Carducci, D. J., and Carducci, J. B. *The Caring Classroom.* Palo Alto, Calif.: Bull Publishing, 1984.

97. Charles, C. W. *Building Classroom Discipline: From Models to Practice.* 3d ed. New York: Longman, 1989.

98. Delgado, J. M. R. "Cerebral Heterostimulation in a Monkey Colony." *Science* 141 (1963): 161–63.

99. Doyle, W. "Classroom Organization and Management." In *Handbook of Research on Teaching*, edited by M. C. Wittrock, 392–431. New York: Macmillan, 1986.

100. Dubelle, S. T., and Hoffman, C. M. *Misbehavin' II.* Lancaster, Pa.: Technomic, 1986.

101. Elam, S. M. "The Second Gallup Phi Delta Kappa Poll of Teachers' Attitudes toward the Public Schools." *Phi Delta Kappan* 70 (1989): 785–98.

102. Emmer, E. T., et al. *Classroom Management for Secondary Teachers.* Englewood Cliffs, N.J.: Prentice-Hall, 1984.

103. Evertson, C. M. "Classroom Organization and Management." In *Knowledge Base for the Beginning Teacher*, edited by M. C. Reynolds, 59–70. Oxford, England: Pergamon Press, 1989.

104. Glasser, W. "10 Steps to Good Discipline." *Today's Education* 60 (1977): 60–63.

105. _____. "Disorders in Our Schools: Causes and Remedies." *Phi Delta Kappan* 59 (1978): 331–33.

106. _____. *Control Theory in the Classroom.* New York: Perennial Library, 1985.

107. Jones, V. F., and Jones, L. S. *Comprehensive Classroom Management.* 2d ed. Boston: Allyn and Bacon, 1986.

108. Kounin, J. *Discipline and Group Management in Classrooms.* New York: Holt, Rinehart & Winston, 1977.

109. Kounin, J., and Sherman, L. "School Environments as Behavior Settings." *Theory into Practice* 18 (1979): 145–51.

110. National Education Association. *Report of the Task Force on Corporal Punishment.* Washington, D.C.: NEA, 1972.

111. Reardon, F. J., and Reynolds, R. N. "A Survey of Attitudes toward Corporal Punishment in Pennsylvania Schools." In *Corporal Punishment in American Education*, edited by I. A. Hyman and J. H. Wise. Philadelphia: Temple University Press, 1979.

112. Rogers, R. L., and McMillin, C. S. *Freeing Someone You Love from Alcohol and Other Drugs: A Step-by-Step Plan Starting Today!* Los Angeles: The Body Press, 1989.

113. Rust, J. O., and Kinnard, K. Q. "Personality Characteristics of the Users of Corporal Punishment in the Schools." *Journal of School Psychology* 21 (1983): 91–105.

114. Shannon, J. "In the Classroom Stoned." *Phi Delta Kappan* 68 (1986): 60–62.

115. Stallion, B. K. "Classroom Management Intervention: The Effects of Mentoring Relationships on the Inductee Teacher's Behavior." Paper presented at annual meeting of American Educational Research Association, New Orleans, 1988.

116. Stanley, S. J., and Popham, W. J., eds. *Teacher Evaluation: Six Perceptions of Success.* Alexandria, Va.: Association for Supervision and Curriculum Development, 1988.

117. Steere, B. F. *Becoming an Effective Classroom Manager: A Resource for Teachers.* Albany, N.Y.: State University of New York Press, 1988.

118. Stiggins, R. J., and Duke, D. *The Case for Commitment to Teacher Growth: Research on Teacher Evaluation.* Albany, N.Y.: State University of New York Press, 1988.

119. Strike, K., and Soltis, J. "'Who Broke the Fish Tank? And Other Ethical Dilemmas." *Instructor* 95 (1986): 36–39.

120. Sulzer-Azaroff, B., and Mayer, G. R. *Applying Behavior Analysis Procedures with Children and Youth.* New York: Holt, Rinehart & Winston, 1977.

121. Towers, R. L. *How Schools Can Help Combat Student Drug and Alcohol Abuse.* Washington, D.C.: National Education Association, 1987.

122. _____. *Children of Alcoholics/Addicts.* Washington, D.C.: National Education Association, 1989.

123. Ulrich, R. E., and Azrin, N. H. "Reflexive Fighting in Response to Aversive Stimulation." *Journal of Experimental Analysis of Behavior* 5 (1962): 511–20.

124. Van Dyke, H. T. "Corporal Punishment in Our Schools." *Clearing House* 57 (1984): 196–300.

125. Weber, W. A. "Classroom Management." In *Classroom Teaching Skills.* 3d ed., edited by J. M. Cooper, 271–357. Lexington, Mass.: D.C. HEATH, 1986.

126. Welsh, R. S. "Spanking: A Grand Old American Tradition?" *Children Today* 14 (1985): 25–29.

127. Wielkiewicz, R. M. *Behavior Management in the Schools: Principles and Procedures.* New York: Pergamon, 1986.

128. Wolfgang, C. H., and Glickman, C. D. *Solving Discipline Problems: Strategies for Classroom Teachers.* 2d ed. Boston: Allyn and Bacon, 1986.

129. Wood, F. H. "The Influence of Public Opinion and Social Custom on the Use of Corporal Punishment in the Schools." In *Punishment and Aversive*

Stimulation in Special Education: Legal, Theoretical, and Practical Issues in Their Use with Emotionally Disturbed Children and Youth, edited by F. H. Wood and K. C. Lakin, 29–39. Reston, Va.: Council for Exceptional Children, 1982.

130. Zumwalt, K., ed. *Improving Teaching: 1986 ASCD Yearbook.* Alexandria, Va.: Association for Supervision and Curriculum Development, 1986.